Warman's

Roseville Pottery

Mark F. Moran

W9-CHP-004

©2004 Krause Publications
Published by

700 East State Street • Iola, WI 54990-0001
715-445-2214 • 888-457-2873
www.krause.com

Our toll-free number to place an order or obtain a free catalog is 800-258-0929.

Library of Congress Catalog Number: 2003111772

ISBN: 0-87349-752-X

Designed by Jamie Griffin
Edited by Dennis Thorton

Printed in USA

Warman's Roseville Pottery

A Six-Decade Experiment

Collectors of Roseville Pottery become quite animated when discussing "experimental" pieces, those with trial glazes or unusual forms that never went into large-scale production.

In fact, the entire 64-year history of the company was one long experiment, first by trying to gauge public tastes, and, finally, by just trying to survive.

Ohio was the center of pottery production in the late 19th century, due to easily accessible waterways and an abundance of raw materials. Natural gas deposits in the Zanesville area, combined with rich clay, provided an ideal foundation for local potteries and gave Zanesville its nickname, "Clay City."

The Roseville Pottery Company, located in Roseville, Ohio, was incorporated on Jan. 4, 1892, with George F. Young as general manager. The company had been producing stoneware since 1890, when it purchased the J. B. Owens Pottery, also of Roseville. Wares included flowerpots and cuspidors, and all were unmarked. "Venetian" baking pans, "German Cooking and Farm Ware," the "Blended" line of jardinières and pedestals, and coin banks and novelties were some of Roseville's earliest products.

The popularity of Roseville Pottery's original lines of stoneware continued to grow. The company acquired new plants in 1892 and 1898, and production started to shift to Zanesville, just a few miles away. By about 1910, all of the work was centered in Zanesville, but the company name was unchanged.

Young hired Ross C. Purdy as artistic designer in 1900, and Purdy created Rozane—a contraction of the words "Roseville" and "Zanesville." Rozane was a style of brown underglaze pottery that was already popular at the time. Rozane was similar to artwares in production at two other Zanesville potteries: Weller Pottery's "Louwelsa" and the Owens Pottery's "Utopian." All of these Zanesville firms were imitating Cincinnati's Rookwood Pottery, which had developed its "Standard Glaze" line in 1884. The first Roseville artware pieces were marked either Rozane or RPCo, both impressed or ink-stamped on the bottom.

In 1902, a line was developed called Azurean, which was similar to Weller's blue Louwelsa: a blue and white underglaze decorated artware on a blended background. Some pieces were marked Azurean, but often RPCO. In 1904 at the St. Louis Exposition, Roseville's Rozane Mongol, a high-gloss oxblood red line, captured first prize,

gaining recognition for the firm and its creator, John Herold.

Other artists included Gazo Fujiyama—who created the Woodland, or Fujiyama, line as well as Rozane Fudji. Many Roseville lines were a response to the innovations of Weller Pottery, and in 1904 Frederick Rhead was hired away from Weller as artistic director. He created the Olympic and Della Robbia lines for Roseville. (He later designed the Fiesta wares for the Homer Laughlin Co.). His brother Harry took over as artistic director in 1908, and in 1915 he introduced the popular Donatello line.

By 1908, all handcrafting ended except for Rozane Royal. Roseville was the first pottery in Ohio to install a tunnel kiln, which increased its production capacity.

Frank Ferrell, who was a top decorator at the Weller Pottery by 1904, was Roseville's artistic director from 1917 until 1954. This Zanesville native created many of the most popular lines, including Pine Cone, which had scores of individual pieces.

Roseville patterns introduced under Ferrell's direction also include:

Futura (1928), Imperial II (1930 glazes), Earlam (1930), Ferella (1930),

Sunflower (circa 1930), Montacello (1931), Windsor (1931), Jonquil (circa 1931), Ivory (1932), Baneda (1932), Blackberry (circa 1932), Cherry Blossom (1933), Tourmaline (1933), Artcraft (1933), Falline (1933), Wisteria (1933), Laurel (1934), Topeo (1934), Luffa (1934), Russco (1934), Velmoss II (1935), Morning Glory (1935), Orian (1935), Clemana (1936), Primrose (1936), Moderne (1936), Moss (1936), Thorn Apple (1937), Dawn (1937), Ixia (1937), Poppy (1938), Teasel (1938), Fuchsia (1938), Iris (1939), Cosmos (1939), Crystal Green (circa 1939), Bleeding Heart (1940), White Rose (1940), Columbine (1941), Rozane Pattern (1941), and Bushberry (1941).

Many collectors believe Roseville's circa 1925 glazes were the best of any Zanesville pottery. George Krause, who had become Roseville's technical supervisor —responsible for glaze—in 1915, remained with Roseville until the 1950s.

Company sales declined after World War II, especially in the early 1950s when cheap Japanese imports began to replace American wares, and a simpler, more modern style made many of Roseville's elaborate floral designs seem old-fashioned.

In the late 1940s, Roseville began to issue lines with glossy glazes (Wincraft, Ming Tree, Artwood, and Lotus). Roseville tried to offset its flagging artware sales by launching a dinnerware line—Raymor—in 1953. Raymor was designed by Ben Siebel, but the style was rather austere when compared to better-selling dinnerware, and the line was a commercial failure.

Roseville issued its last new designs in 1953. On Nov. 29, 1954, the facilities of Roseville were sold to the Mosaic Tile Company.

Condition and Pricing

Since many of the Roseville pieces listed in this book were sold at auction, the descriptions are very detailed, down to the length of hairlines and the position of "flea-bite" nicks. Most price guides list values assuming a piece is in mint condition, but the prices here reflect the reality that very few examples of pottery survive for decades without at least minor wear or damage.

Reproductions

Since the mid-1990s, Roseville Pottery fakes and reproductions have been a growing problem. The best way to learn about reproductions is to visit The Roseville Exchange, whose motto is "dedicated to helping the public spot reproduction (fake) Roseville Pottery." You can find it online at http://www.ohioriverpottery.com/roseville_exchange/roseville.html. The site offers information on hundreds of reproductions—with style numbers and images—contributed by collectors, and side-by-side comparisons with real pieces.

Words of Thanks

This book would not have been possible without the generosity of:

David Rago Auctions,
333 N. Main St.,
Lambertville, NJ 08530.
Phone: (609) 397-9374.
Fax: (609) 397-9377.
Web site: http://www.ragoarts.com/.
E-mail: info@ragoarts.com.

The Iridescent House,
227 First Ave. SW,
Rochester, MN 55902.
Phone: (507) 288-0320.
Web site: http://www.iridescenthouse.com.

Adamstown Antique Gallery,
2000 N. Reading Rd.,
Denver, PA 17517.
Phone: (717) 335-3435.
Web site: http://www.aagal.com/.

Antiques of Red Wing,
307 Main St.,
Red Wing, MN 55066.
Phone: (651) 385-5963.
E-mail: antiquesofrw@mcleodusa.net.

Memory Maker Antiques,
415 Main St.,
Red Wing, MN 55066.
Phone: (651) 385-5914.

Carlson s Antiques
Bill and Sliv Carlson
Wayzata, Minn.
(952) 475-0586
http://CarlsonsAntiques.com/
Bill@CarlsonsAntiques.com

Bottom Marks

There is no consistency to Roseville bottom marks. Even within a single popular pattern like Pine Cone, the marks vary.

Several shape numbering systems were implemented during the company's 64-year history, with some denoting a vessel style and some applied to separate lines. Though many pieces are unmarked, from 1900 until the late teens or early 1920s, Roseville used a variety of marks including "RPCo," "Roseville Pottery Company," and the word "Rozane," the last often with a line name, i.e., "Egypto."

The underglaze ink script "Rv" mark was used on lines introduced from the mid-to-late teens through the mid-1920s. Around 1926 or 1927, Roseville began to use a small, triangular black paper label on lines such as Futura and Imperial II. Silver or gold foil labels began to appear around 1930, continuing for several years on lines such as Blackberry and Tourmaline, and on some early Pine Cone.

From 1932 to 1937, an impressed script mark was added to the molds used on new lines, and around 1937 the raised script mark was added to the molds of new lines. The relief mark includes "U.S.A."

All bottom mark images appear courtesy Adamstown Antique Gallery, Adamstown, Pennsylvania.

Impressed mark on Azurean vase, 8" tall.

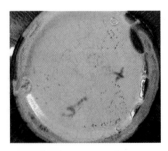

Faint ink stamps on Baneda green vessel.

Gold foil label on Baneda pink vase.

Raised mark on Bushberry green ewer.

Raised mark on Bushberry vase

Grease pencil marks on Carnelian II vase, 14" tall.

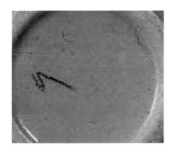

Ink mark on Cherry Blossom pink vase, 10" tall.

Raised mark on Cosmos blue floor vase, 18" tall.

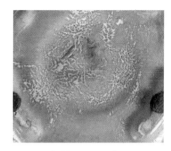

Faint mark (?) on Crystalis squat vessel, 4" tall.

Impressed numeral on Crocus urn, 6" tall.

Side-marked initials (possibly Harry Larzelere) on Della Robbia vase, 7" tall.

Wafer mark on Della Robbia vase, 10 1/2" tall.

Wafer mark on Della Robbia vase, 10" tall.

Wafer on Egypto ewer, 11" tall.

Wafer on Egypto vase, 9" tall.

Grease pencil marks on Falline spherical vase, 6" tall.

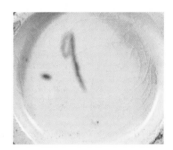

Ink mark on Falline bulbous vase, 7" tall.

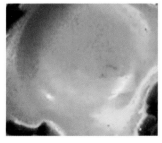

Unmarked base of Ferella vase, 6" tall.

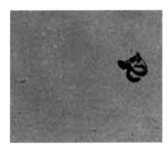

Ink stamp on Florentine I 10" jardinière.

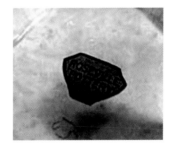

Black paper label on Futura footed vessel, 4 1/2" tall.

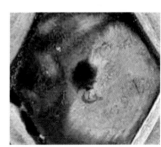

Obscured ink stamp on Hexagon vase, 5" tall.

Marks on Imperial II squat vessel.

Gold foil label and grease pencil marks on Imperial II vase, 10" tall.

Impressed mark on Iris vase.

Raised mark on Lotus vase in a trial glaze, 10" tall.

Faint impressed mark on Mara vase, 8" tall.

Obscured marks on Morning Glory vase, 10" tall.

Ink stamp on Panel vase with nudes, 10" tall.

Impressed mark on Pine Cone blue cider pitcher.

Gold foil label on Pine Cone blue spherical planter.

Raised mark on Pine Cone blue pillow vase.

Impressed and incised marks on Pine Cone blue vase.

Faint impressed and ink marks on Pine Cone blue vase.

Impressed mark on Pine Cone green footed planter.

Impressed marks on Rozane portrait vase, 13" tall.

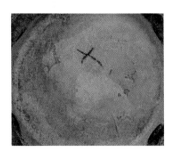

Marks on Russco bulbous urn, 6 1/2" tall.

Raised mark and ink stamp on Silhouette brown vase.

Raised mark and ink stamp on Silhouette red vase.

Faint mark on Sunflower bulbous vessel, 4" tall.

Faint ink stamp and grease pencil on Velmoss pink vase.

Raised mark on Water Lily brown floor vase.

Raised mark on Wincraft cylindrical panther vase, 11" tall.

Mark on Windsor bulbous vessel.

Ink stamps on Wisteria bowl, 5" tall.

Faint ink stamp on Wisteria bulbous vase, 8" tall.

Apple Blossom

Introduced in 1948, this pattern features irregular leafy apple branches—some of which form handles—with clusters of white blossoms on blue, green, and pink-orange backgrounds. The pieces have raised marks with style numbers.

Apple Blossom blue basket
(316-15″), raised mark.

$250-$300

Seven Apple Blossom blue pieces
pair of low candlesticks, hanging basket, center bowl, basket, dish, and vase, all marked.

$500-$600/set

Apple Blossom blue tea set
(371), raised marks; teapot: 7″ by 11″.

$550-$650

Apple Blossom blue vase
(393-18″), raised mark.

$1,200-$1,400

Apple Blossom blue ewer
(318-15″), raised mark, 15 1/2″ by 5 1/2″ by 4 3/4″.

$1,000-$1,200

Apple Blossom blue wall pocket
(366-8˝).

$200-$250

Three Apple Blossom pieces
blue bowl, (nicked) pink bowl (329-10˝), and pink basket (310-10˝), all marked.

$325-$375/set

Two Apple Blossom pieces
pink rectangular planter (368-8˝) and blue jardinière (301-6˝) with small chips and hairlines, both marked.

$90-$110/pair

Apple Blossom green basket
(310-10˝), raised mark.

$200-$250

Apple Blossom green jardinière
(303-10˝) and pedestal (306-10˝), jardinière has several chips at base and flakes to flowers, normal abrasion to top of pedestal, both marked.

$450-$550

Apple Blossom green jardinière
(303-10˝), glaze chip and bruise to base and some small glaze flakes to petals, raised mark.

$175-$225

Four Apple Blossom green pieces
jardinière (803-10˝) with drilled bottom, vase (382-7˝) with bruise to base, and a pair of candlesticks (351), all marked.

$250-$300/set

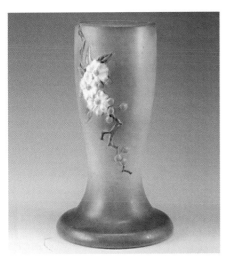

Apple Blossom green pedestal
(300-10″), raised mark.

$110-$140

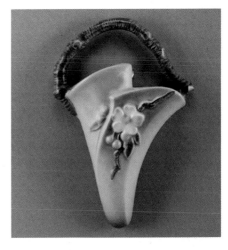

Apple Blossom green vase with squat base
(388-10″), raised mark.

$150-$200

Apple Blossom green wall pocket
(366-8″), repair to handle (some flaking of paint), raised mark.

$110-$140

Apple Blossom pink hanging basket
repair to rim chip and light abrasion to decoration, 5 1/2″ by 8″.

$90-$110

Apple Blossom pink creamer and sugar
(371-C and 371-S), raised marks.

$150-$175/pair

Apple Blossom pink jardinière
(301-6″), raised mark, 6 1/4″ by 8 1/2″.

$225-$275

Apple Blossom pink tea set
(371), all marked.

$375-$425/set

Apple Blossom pink pillow vase
(390-12″), flat chip to base, raised mark.
$125-$175

Two Apple Blossom pink vases
pillow vase (373-7″) with small chip to bottom ring, and taller vase (385-8″), raised marks.
$175-$225/pair

Apple Blossom pink vase
(389-10″), raised mark, 10 1/8″ by 4 3/4″ by 6″.
$350-$400

Four Apple Blossom pink pieces
pair of planters (300-4″), rectangular planter (368-8″), and fan vase (373-7″), all marked.
$325-$375/set

Artcraft

Introduced in 1933, Artcraft combined art deco influences and usually the earth tones of green and brownish tan, sometimes blue-green, occasionally with shades of pink and dull gold. The sleek, simple design features blunt buttressed supports and squat bases on the jardinières. The pieces are unmarked or have a foil label.

Artcraft pedestal
covered in shaded blue and green matte glazes, underglaze chip to base, and a few minute flecks to rim, unmarked, 17″ by 9″.

$900-$1,100

Artcraft jardinière covered in a shaded green, rose, and yellow matte glaze, spider lines to base, chips to foot ring, and line from rim, 7″ by 10″.

$250-$300

Artcraft jardinière
with four buttresses at the shoulder, exterior in light green and mottled blue, tan interior, 4 1/4″ by 5 3/4″.

$400-$450

Two Artcraft jardinières
in a mottled brown and green glaze, 3″ V-shaped line from rim of one, unmarked, 7″ diameter and 5 1/2″ diameter.

$375-$425/pair

Artcraft jardinière
in an Earlam glaze of mottled turquoise and lavender with a tan interior, unmarked, 4 1/8″ tall.

$450-$550

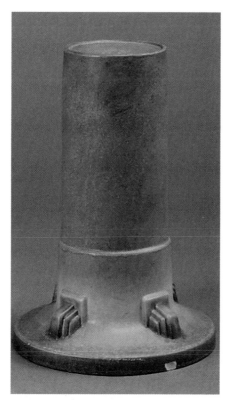

Artcraft brown pedestal
3/4″ chip to base, two small glaze flakes to top, and short tight line, unmarked, 17″ by 11″.

$450-$500

Artcraft brown planter
foil label, 5″ by 7 1/4″.

$200-$250

Two green Artcraft jardinières
silver foil label on one, 9 1/2″ diameter and 5 1/2″ diameter.
$750-$850/pair

Artcraft jardinière
in an oxblood glaze typical of the Topeo or Mowa
lines, unmarked, 6 1/8″ tall.
$700-$800

Pair of small Artcraft jardinières
with atypical black and white glazes, unmarked,
white is 4 1/4″ tall, black is 4″ tall.
$500-$600 each

Artware and Landscape

Decorated Artware and Landscape pieces reflect the art nouveau influence at the turn of the 19th century. Designs included glossy, idealized landscapes with birds, and fruit and floral motifs. The highly stylized motifs in the Landscape line were created both with squeeze-bag decoration and layers of clay (sgraffito), and most were found on jardinières, pedestals, and umbrella stands. None are marked.

Landscape jardinière and pedestal
by Fredrick H. Rhead, decorated in squeeze-bag
with flying geese over stylized fruit trees on the
jardinière, and a landscape with stone wall on the
pedestal. Jardinière has restoration to several chips
and 5″ V-shaped hairline from rim, overpainting
around base (possibly from lifting overglaze), and
several minor nicks to squeeze-bag; pedestal has
restoration to 6″ crack from top, and damage to
overglaze on horizontal line halfway around neck;
both pieces marked with artist's cipher; jardinière:
12 1/2″ by 18″, pedestal: 29″ by 13 3/4″.
$1,500-$1,700

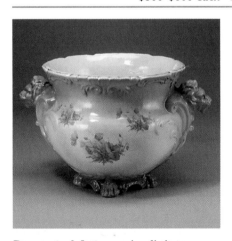

Decorated Artware jardiniere
painted with red poppies on a shaded green,
ochre and ivory ground, embossed with lion heads
forming two handles; some flaking, nicks, and
lines, unmarked, 12″ by 16″.
$150-$200

Decorated Landscape jardinière
with stylized trees and flying bird (456), 6 5/8″ tall.
$450-$550

Artwood

Introduced in 1951, Artwood's most significant feature is the irregularly shaped opening in the sides of vessels—referred to by the company as "picture" elements—which are pierced by tree branches or flowers. The glossy mottled glazes include yellow, brown, green, blue, gray, and lavender. pieces are marked "Roseville U.S.A."

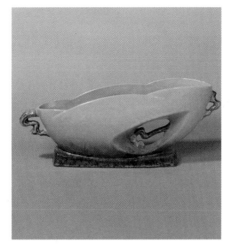

Artwood oval planter
with cherry blossom branch (1062-12″), covered in a glossy brown and yellow glaze, raised mark.
$350-$400

Two Artwood circular vases with branches
(1053-8″), raised marks.
$250-$300/pair

Artwood gray three-piece planter
set consisting of an Ikebana vase (1051-6″) decorated with nasturtium (minor flat nick under base) and two small side sections (1050), raised marks.
$300-$350/set

Artwood gray Ikebana flaring vase
(1057-8″), decorated with a chestnut branch, raised mark.
$250-$300

Artwood gray vase with yellow tulips
(1056-10″), raised mark.
$200-$250

Artwood green vase with pinecones
(1060-12″), raised mark.
$250-$300

Artwood yellow circular vase
(1053-8″) with tight line from rim, raised mark.
$60-$80

Artwood Ikebana vase with thistle
(1059-10″), covered in a glossy green and brown glaze, raised mark.

$400-$450

Artwood yellow ikebana vase with thistle
(1059-10″), minor flake to inner rim, raised mark.

$80-$100

Artwood Ikebana vase
(1056-10″) with tulip under a yellow, brown, and green glaze, raised mark.

$90-$110

Artwood Ikebana vase with cypress tree
(1052-8″), covered in a glossy yellow and brown glaze, raised mark.

$250-$300

Artwood Ikebana vase
(1055-9″) decorated with an oak branch, and covered in a glossy green and brown glaze, raised mark.

$450-$500

Autumn

Circa 1912, Autumn is a line of jardinières, planters, pitchers, basins, and chamber pots, all with transfer decoration of deciduous trees against a woodland landscape. The typical color combination is a blend of yellow with glossy red-orange or terra-cotta rims and bases, but other hues—including blues, greens and pinks—are known. Fewer than 20 shapes have been identified, and are usually unmarked.

Autumn jardinière
(480-10″), unmarked.

$350-$450

Aztec

Introduced in 1904 and strongly influenced by the art nouveau movement, the name "Aztec" is a misnomer. This line featured stylized floral and geometric designs—with the occasional ship or Moorish arches—applied with slip cup or squeeze bag. Background colors include blue (from pale to navy), russet, gray, ivory, teal, and tan. Most are unmarked.

Aztec blue pitcher
unmarked, 5 1/2″ by 7″.
$550-$650

Two Aztec pieces
tall flaring vase with white and beige flowers on brown stems against a light blue ground (several chips around base, glaze scaling all around rim, and 3″ line), and a squat pitcher with stylized pattern in dark green and white on a dark blue ground (restoration to spout and to base), unmarked, 11″ by 5″ and 5 1/4″ by 7 1/2″.
$200-$250/pair

Aztec bulbous vase
slip-decorated with band of spade-shaped flowers in polychrome against a powder blue ground, over-firing to area on body and around rim, restoration to chips at base, unmarked, 6 1/2″ by 4 1/2″.
$175-$225

Aztec corseted vase
with trillium squeeze-bag detail, glaze scaling to rim and base, one fleck to decoration, unmarked, 8 1/4″ by 3 3/4″.
$250-$300

Aztec blue trumpet-shaped vase
decorated in polychrome squeeze bag with a garland pattern, light abrasion to some spots on white decoration, unmarked, 11″ by 5″.
$275-$325

Aztec ovoid vase
(No. 7) in blue glaze with stylized floral decoration, Rozane Ware wafer, 10″ tall.
$450-$500

Aztec trumpet vase
1/4″ glaze flake to base and very minor flecks to squeeze-bag details, unmarked, 11 1/4″ by 5 1/2″.
$250-$300

Two Aztec vases
one tapering with flat rim by E.C., decorated with stylized crocuses in yellow and green on a teal ground (two chips to rim with 2″ V-shaped line from one), and one bulbous decorated with stylized swags in white, yellow, and green on a blue ground (several hairlines from rim and several nicks to high points), first one has Rozane Ware wafer, 9″ by 4″ and 8″ by 3 1/2″.
$500-$600/pair

Aztec vase
with bulbous shoulder and tapering body, decorated with stylized flowers and swags in white, yellow, and blue on a blue-gray ground, some burst bubbles and some minor nicks, unmarked, 11″ by 4 1/2″.

$350-$400

Two Aztec vases
right: shape No. 7 in dusty blue with stylized foral decoration, 10 1/2″ tall, unmarked,
$450-$550;
left: shape No. 4 in taupe with geometric decoration in cream and blue, unmarked, 10 1/4″ tall.

$400-$500

Three Aztec vases
right: shape No. 15 in blue with art nouveau line decoration in cream and gray, unmarked, 9 3/4″ tall,
$350-$450;
center, shape No. 20 in tan with art nouveau line decoration in cream and blue, unmarked, 9 1/4″ tall,
$400-$450;
left, shape No. 24 in blue-gray with art nouveau line decoration in cream and gray, unmarked, 7 7/8″ tall.

$350-$450

Azurean

Introduced shortly after the turn of the 19th century, this line featured hand-painted scenes or floral motifs done in varying shades of blue on a shaded white background. Many are signed by the artist and/or marked with an impressed "RPCo."

Azurean trumpet-shaped vase
decorated by F.S. with fishermen in their boats, restoration to top, stamped "865/RPCo./2.," 18″ by 6 1/2″.

$1,400-$1,600

Courtesy Adamstown Antique Gallery

Azurean vase
decorated with fishing boats, 8″ by 3″.

$2,000-$2,100

Two Azurean vases
both painted with flowers, both with indistinct marks right: two-handled, 8 1/4″ tall.

$900-$1,000

left, ovoid, 6 3/8″ tall.

$450-$550

Baneda

Introduced in 1932, the name comes from the design motif which features a wide band that encloses spiky leaves, vines, and pods, often in dripping glazes of green, blue, orange, and yellow. Backgrounds are mainly green or pink, rarely blue. Pieces are unmarked or have a foil label.

Baneda green jardinière
unmarked, 4″ by 5 1/2″.

$350-$400

Baneda green low bowl
with crisp mold and good color, unmarked, 7 1/2″ diameter.

$350-$400

Baneda green jardinière
with crisp mold and good color, unmarked, 8″ by 11 1/2″.

$2,400-$2,600

Baneda green candlesticks
restoration to one handle, foil labels, sample tag, and John Wanamaker store tags, 5 1/4″ by 3 1/2″.

$450-$550

Large Baneda green jardinière
with strong mold, extensive professional restoration, unmarked.

$800-$1,000

Baneda green bulbous urn
with strong mold, unmarked, 6 1/4" by 4".
$600-$700

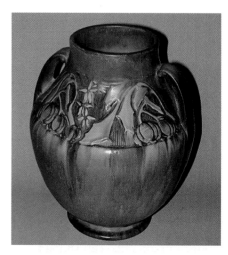

Baneda green bulbous urn
bruise and restored chip to rim, crisp mold, good
color, unmarked, 10" by 9".
$800-$900

Baneda green footed vase
unmarked, 7" by 5 1/2".
$750-$850

Baneda green bulbous vase
with very strong mold and color; two flat chips to
foot ring (do not show on side), unmarked, 15 3/4"
by 7 3/4".
$3,200-$3,300

Baneda green flaring vase
unmarked, 8 1/2" by 5 1/2".
$800-$900

Baneda green flaring vase
with good mold, glaze pimple to rim, unmarked,
12 1/4" by 7 1/4".
$1,100-$1,300

Baneda green milk-can shaped vase
very tight bruise and opposing short hairlines to rim, unmarked, 7 1/4″ by 5 3/4″.

$350-$400

Baneda green vase
foil label, 7″ tall.

$400-$450

Baneda green spherical vase
unmarked, 5 1/2″ by 6 1/2″.

$700-$800

Baneda green bulbous vessel
with collared rim and good mold and color, black paper label, 9 1/2″ by 5″.

$1,500-$1,700

Baneda green squat vessel
foil label, 6 3/4″ by 7″.

$500-$600

Baneda pink faceted bowl
with 1″ bruise to one handle, silver foil label, 3 1/4″ by 11″.

$350-$400

Baneda pink candlesticks
unmarked, 5 1/2″ by 3 1/2″.

$450-$500/pair

Baneda pink planter
small, with good mold, pock mark, unmarked, 4 1/4″ by 5 1/2″.

$275-$325

Baneda pink bulbous urn
with strong mold and color, 1/2″ crazing line to rim, foil label, 7″ by 7″.

$400-$500

Baneda pink bulbous urn
with very strong mold and color, silver foil label,
9 1/4″ by 7 3/4″.

$850-$950

Baneda pink urn
with crisp mold and color, unmarked, 12 1/4″ by
9 3/4″.

$1,300-$1,500

Baneda pink bulbous vase
with strong mold, black paper label, 6 1/4″ by 4″.

$400-$500

Baneda pink milk-can shaped vase
with strong mold, unmarked, 7″ tall.

$450-$550

Baneda pink ovoid vase
silver foil label, 6 1/4″ by 3 1/2″.

$350-$450

Baneda pink pear-shaped vase
minor bruise to one handle, unmarked, 5 1/2″ by
4 1/2″.

$250-$300

Baneda pink flaring vase
with strong mold, unmarked, 7 1/4″ by 4 1/4″.

$550-$650

Baneda pink bulbous vessel
foil label, 4 1/4″ by 4 1/2″.

$250-$300

Baneda pink flaring wall pocket
restoration to chip at rim, and short, tight firing
line to back, unmarked, 8 1/4″ by 7 1/2″.

$1,900-$2,100

Banks

Because they were usually given to youngsters, these banks rarely survived without some damage, and many were broken to get at the money inside. Dating from the early 1900s, shapes included cats, dogs, pigs, birds, and even a buffalo and Uncle Sam. They were simply and crudely glazed in mottled brown, yellow, green, and red, and were unmarked.

Three early banks
one of Uncle Sam, one monkey on a chamber pot, and one jug inscribed "Ye Olden Time" (minor fleck to rim), in assorted glazes, unmarked; 4 3/4″ by 3 1/2″, 5 3/4″ by 3″, and 4 1/4″ by 3 1/2″.

$350-$400/set

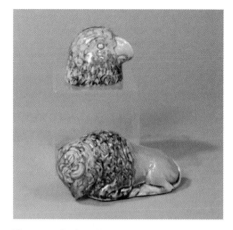

Two early banks
one of an eagle's head marked "Souvenir/ Sheboygan, Wis." on a mottled yellow and green ground, and one buffalo in mottled beige, unmarked, 2 3/4″ by 3 1/2″, and 3 1/4″ by 6″.

$400-$500/pair

Bittersweet

Like the invasive deciduous perennial, Bittersweet pieces are wrapped in leafy green vines with reddish-yellow flowers and woody handles. Introduced in 1951, backgrounds are gray, green, and yellow; the mark is usually raised.

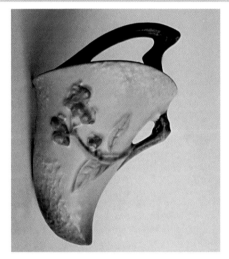

Bittersweet wall pocket
unmarked, 7″ by 4 5/8″ by 2 1/2″.

$400-$500

Bittersweet footed vase
(863-4″), 6″ by 4 1/8″ by 5 3/8″.

$150-$200

Bittersweet yellow wall pocket
(866-7″), small flake to foot, raised mark.

$150-$200

Two Bittersweet vases
(885-10″), one gray and one yellow, both marked.

$300-$350/pair

Bittersweet yellow tea set
(871) with small nick to decoration on teapot, crack to lid of sugar, and small nick to bowl, raised marks; teapot: 7 1/4″ by 11″.

$200-$250/set

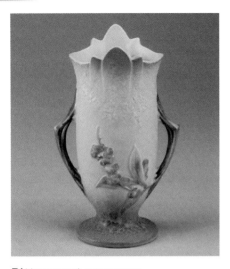

Bittersweet gray vase
(885-10˝), raised mark.

$125-$175

Two Bittersweet yellow pieces
basket (810-10˝) and cornucopia-shaped vase (822-8˝), raised marks.

$275-$325/pair

Two Bittersweet pieces
gray vase (885-10˝) with restoration to rim tip, and green basket (808-6˝) with reglued chip to base, raised marks.

$125-$175/pair

Four Bittersweet pieces
gray basket (808-6˝), yellow vase (885-10˝), green basket (810-10˝) with chips and cracked handle, and small bowl (826-6˝), all marked.

$275-$325/set

Three Bittersweet vessels
green double planter (858), yellow pillow vase (884-8˝), and yellow planter (841-5˝), all marked.

$275-$325/set

Blackberry

Introduced about 1932, this line features a collar of russet and green leaves, dark blue berries, and a textured background in varying shades of brown and green. The pieces are unmarked or have foil or paper labels.

Blackberry low bowl
strong color, minor glaze bubbles, minute pinprick to rim, unmarked, 3 1/4″ by 7 3/4″.

$250-$300

Blackberry basket
very small nick to one berry, unmarked, rare, 7 1/2″ by 6″.

$1,000-$1,100

Blackberry faceted low bowl
with strong mold, foil label, 3 1/2″ by 13 1/2″.
$600-$700

Blackberry pair of candlesticks
with good mold and color, gold foil label to one, 4 1/2″ by 4″.

$500-$600

Blackberry faceted planter
unmarked, 3 1/2″ by 9 3/4″.

$300-$375

Blackberry spherical planter
with two short rim handles, 1/2″ chip to inner part of one handle, small bruise to rim, unmarked, 6 1/4″ by 7 1/2″.

$350-$400

Blackberry spherical planter
black paper label, 4 3/4″ by 4″.

$350-$450

Blackberry bulbous urn
with collared rim, strong mold, minute fleck to rim,
two stilt-pull chips, unmarked, 12 1/4″ by 8 1/4″.

$900-$1,000

Blackberry vase
4″ line from rim, unmarked, 6 1/4″ by 5 1/2″.

$300-$350

**Two Blackberry
vases**
the larger with restored
inner rim chip, the
smaller with burst
bubbles throughout,
unmarked, 6 1/4″ tall
and 5 1/4″ tall.

$375-$425/pair

Blackberry bulbous vase
(#575) with good mold, unmarked, 8 1/4″ by 5 1/4″.

$600-$700

Blackberry vase
with crisp mold and good color, unmarked, 6 1/4"
by 5 1/2".

$500-$600

Blackberry bulbous two-handled vase
touch-up to fleck on one handle, unmarked, 5" by
4 3/4".

$225-$275

Blackberry bulbous vessel
strong mold and color, black paper label, 5 1/4" by
4 1/2".

$400-$500

Blackberry shouldered vessel
unmarked, 6 1/4" by 5 1/2".

$400-$500

Blackberry squat vessel
unmarked, 4 1/2" by 6".

$300-$350

Blackberry flaring wall pocket
unmarked, 7 3/4" tall.

$1,200-$1,400

Bleeding Heart

Introduced in 1940, the pink flowers and pale or mottled green leaves stretch across backgrounds that include blue, green, and pink. This pattern has a raised mark: "Roseville U.S.A."

Bleeding Heart blue basket
(360-10"), raised mark.

$350-$400

Pair of Bleeding Heart blue book-shaped bookends
(6"), soft mold, one has restoration to corner, raised marks.

$550-$650/pair

Two Bleeding Heart blue pieces
faceted vase (968-8˝) and cornucopia (141-6˝),
raised marks.

$850-$950/pair

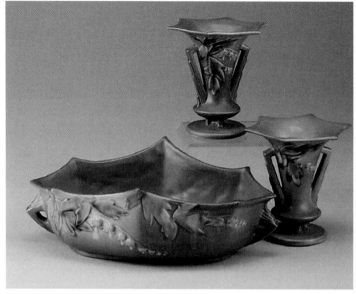

Three Bleeding Heart blue pieces
bowl (382-10˝) and a pair of flaring vases (962-5˝), all marked.

$350-$400/set

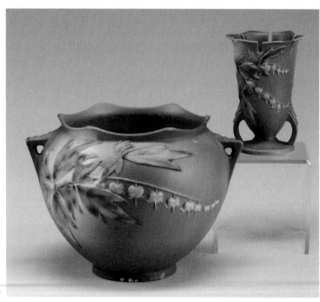

Two Bleeding Heart blue pieces
bulbous planter (as-is condition: chips, cracks, drilled hole) and vase (964-6˝), both marked, planter: 8˝ tall.

$150-$200/pair

Bleeding Heart blue corseted vase
with squat base (969-8˝), raised mark.

$750-$850

Two Bleeding Heart blue pieces
flaring vase (964-6˝) and small jardinière (651-3˝), crisp molds, raised marks.

$600-$700/pair

Two Bleeding Heart ewers
one blue (972-10˝) with crisp mold, and one green (963-6˝), raised marks.

$650-$750/pair

Bleeding Heart green footed basket
with buttressed base and attached flower frog (361-12˝), small chip to frog, raised mark.

$500-$600

Bleeding Heart blue tapering vase
(976-15″), 1/2″ bruise to bottom, raised mark.
$650-$750

Three Bleeding Heart pieces
a pink jardinière (651-3″), and a pair of green vases (962-5″) with repair to one tip, all marked.
$175-$225/set

Two Bleeding Heart pieces
green double bud vase (140-4 1/2″) and blue center bowl (382-10″) with small flake to one handle and to one rim tip, raised marks.

$300-$350/pair

Bleeding Heart pink floor vase
(977-18″), restoration to two points on rim, small chips to inner base ring (do not show on side), raised mark, rare.

$325-$375

Blended

Though sometimes called majolica, that name does not really capture the frequent linear and swirling themes of the Blended line, introduced in the early 1900s. The colors, however, are similar to majolica hues, and were applied to jardinières, pedestals, and sand and umbrella holders. Pieces are often unmarked or occasionally have incised marks.

Blended Iris jardinière
as-is condition (lines, bruises, chips), unmarked, 11″ by 12″.

$300-$350

Blended jardinière
(422) in streaked maroon and charcoal glazes, unmarked, 11 1/2″ tall.

$350-$400

Blended jardinière and pedestal
(414), each with embossed lion's head handles and covered in a brown, green, and yellow flambé majolica glaze, some hairlines and several chips to both pieces, unmarked; jardinière: 12 3/4″ by 20″, pedestal: 21″ by 13″.

$500-$600

Blended jardinière
(479) in dripping rose, yellow, and green glazes with a raised design of stylized flowers and vines, unmarked, 8″ tall.

$250-$300

Blended jardinière
(458) with a motif of swimming fish in a green glaze, unmarked, 8″ tall.

$250-$300

Blended umbrella stand
impressed with stylized arches under a brown, yellow, and forest green majolica glaze, a few shallow scratches and minor pockmarks to decoration, incised mark "727," 20 1/4″ by 9 1/4″.

$375-$425

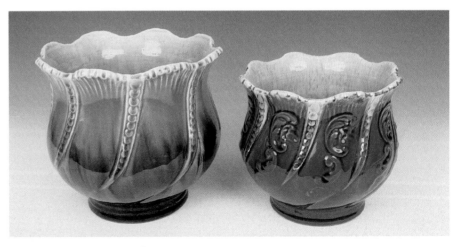

Pair of Blended jardinières
left, (406) in raspberry and turquoise, 6 5/8″ tall, $125 - $150; right, (407) in cobalt and chartreuse, 5 3/4″ tall.

$100-$125

Burmese

Featuring stoic-faced male and female heads in green, black, or ivory, the Burmese line from 1950 included bookends, sconces, and candleholders. Pieces usually have raised marks.

Two Burmese green wall plaques
(72-B and 82-B), raised marks, 8˝ tall.
$350-$375/pair

Pair of Burmese black sconces
(80-B), raised marks, 8˝ tall.
$175-$200/pair

Two Burmese green sconces
(80-B), raised marks, 8˝ tall.
$200-$225/pair

Bushberry

Introduced in 1941, Bushberry has large three-section leaves with sawtooth edges and clusters of berries. The handles are stylized branch forms, and the textured background colors are blue, brown (really more of a terra cotta red), and green. Pieces feature raised marks.

Bushberry blue basket
(370-8˝), with crisp mold, raised mark.
$175-$225

Bushberry blue basket
(371-10˝), raised mark.
$275-$325

Bushberry blue three-piece tea set
teapot (2-T), creamer (2-C), and sugar dish (2-S), chips to sugar dish and creamer, and minute fleck to berry on teapot, raised marks; teapot: 6˝ by 10 1/2˝.
$225-$275/set

Three Bushberry blue pieces
cylindrical vase with twisted handles (32-7″), with restoration to very minor flat chip at base, and two cups (1- 3 1/2″), one with line from rim, all marked.

$175-$225/set

Three Bushberry pieces
blue cornucopia-shaped vase (154-8″), brown teapot (2-T) with abrasion to spout and missing lid, and blue planter (657-4″), all marked.

$125-$175/set

Bushberry brown basket
(370-8″), some very minor nicks at base, raised mark.

$125-$175

Bushberry brown basket
(372-12″), large repair to chips at base, two reglued cracks to handle, two small chips to handle, raised mark, unusual form.

$110-$140

Bushberry brown tea set
(2) with small underglaze chip to base of sugar bowl, raised marks; teapot: 6 1/2″ by 10 3/4″.

$300-$400/set

Bushberry brown double cornucopia vase
(155-8″), raised mark, 8 3/8″ by 5″ by 6 1/8″.

$175-$225

Bushberry brown handled vase
(31-7˝), 7 3/4˝ by 5 3/8˝ by 4 1/2˝.

$225-$275

Bushberry brown small planter
(657-3˝), raised mark, 4 5/8˝ by 3˝.

$125-$150

Four Bushberry brown pieces
basket (370-8˝) with crack to handle, small planter
(657-3˝) with repaired base and fleck to handle, flat
vase (36-9˝) with fleck to leaf, and bowl (416-12˝)
with three flecks to rim, all marked.

$300-$350/set

Three Bushberry pieces
brown bud vase (152-7˝) with nicks at base and a
pair of blue vases (35-9˝), with nick to berry and
repair to chip at base of one, raised marks.

$250-$300/set

Bushberry green basket
(371-10˝), 1/4˝ chip to rim, and repaired lines and
nicks to handle, raised mark.

$110-$140

Bushberry green creamer
(2-C) and sugar bowl (2-S), raised marks.

$90-$110/pair

Bushberry green planter
(384-8˝), raised mark, 12˝ by 3 1/2˝ by 3 1/2˝.

$200-$250

Bushberry green planter
(778-14″), flat chip and bruise to base, raised mark.
$900-$1,100

Two Bushberry vases
with crisp molds, one green (37-10″) and one blue (32-7″), several nicks and bruises overall, raised marks.

$275-$325/pair

Bushberry green floor vase
(41-18″), some small flat chips to base, light glaze scaling, and minor bruise to one berry, raised mark.

$350-$450

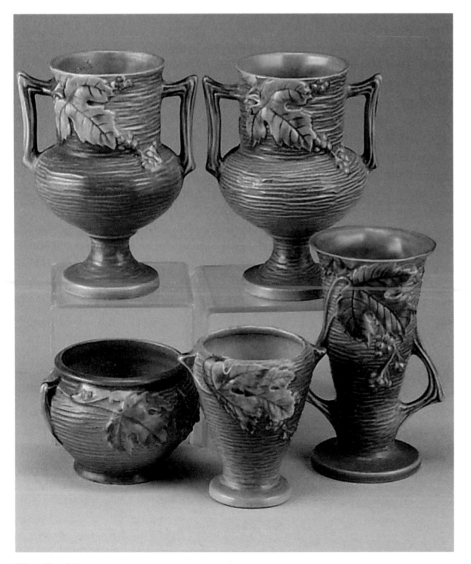

Five Bushberry vases
three blue and two green (28-4″, 156-6″, 30-6″, 657-3″); restoration to rim of one, and bruise to base of another, all marked.

$400-$450/set

Bushberry green vase
(37-10″), strong mold and color, small chip to one berry, raised mark.

$225-$275

Cameo I and II

The Cameo motif (circa 1910) featured two distinct themes: females in profile in a woodland setting, and a classical Greek scene with horsemen, all on jardinières and pedestals. The pieces seen here are identified as Cameo II or Cherub. Both Cameo I and II are unmarked.

Cameo II vase
with cherubs and columns, in green brown and ivory glazes, bruise to one nose, unmarked, 8″ by 4 1/4″.

$175-$225

Three Cameo II vases
with cherubs and columns, in green, brown, and ivory glazes, all unmarked, left: 8″ tall; center, 9 7/8″ tall; right, 7 7/8″ tall.

$300-$400 each

Cameo II jardinière
with cherubs and columns, in green, brown, and ivory glazes, unmarked, 9″ tall.

$400-$500

Capri

From 1950, Capri was made in vivid glossy or mottled colors in shapes that were borrowed both from nature and from the period taste for sleek and sinuous forms. Pieces have raised marks.

Six Capri pieces
four dishes (527-7″) and two planters (558), in assorted glazes, all marked; planters: 7″ by 6″.

$200-$250/set

Carnelian I and II

Carnelian I and II are distinctly different in both shape and color. Carnelian I, circa 1910, has dripping glazes in shapes based on classical vessels. Colors include gray, dull green, blue, and a yellow that's more of an ochre. Ink stamps are common, but some are unmarked.

Carnelian II, circa 1915, are generally heavier and simpler in appearance and the mottled, dripping glazes include amber, green, purple, red, pink, teal, and mauve. Pieces are unmarked or have a paper label.

Unusual Carnelian I-shape bulbous vase
covered in an experimental turquoise, gray, and brown dripping glaze, "Rv" ink stamp, 7" tall.

$400-$500

Carnelian I tall ewer
in gray and buff, restoration to spout, "Rv" ink stamp, 15 1/4" tall.

$225-$275

Carnelian I green ovoid vase
with restoration to chip at base, "Rv" ink stamp, 10 1/4" tall.

$90-$110

Carnelian I spherical vase
covered in a dripping green glaze over a pale pink ground, restoration to chip at rim, "Rv" ink stamp, 8 1/4" by 10 1/2".

$125-$175

Carnelian I handled vase
tan over pale green glaze (319-9"), bottom ink stamp "Rv," 9 1/2" by 9".

$450-$525

Three Carnelian I yellow pieces
a pair of candle holders and a vase (1/4″ chip at rim), "Rv″ ink stamp on all; candleholders are 3″ tall each, vase 4 1/2″ tall.

$125-$175/set

Carnelian I vase
with buttressed supports, dark green dripping glaze on pale green body, unmarked, 6″ by 5 1/8″ by 4″.

$150-$175

Two Carnelian I pieces
blue wall pocket in as-is condition (chips, lines), and a yellow vase, "Rv″ ink stamp to both; vase: 10 1/4″ tall.

$125-$175/pair

Two Carnelian I yellow bulbous vases
"Rv″ ink stamp to both, 8″ and 7″.

$275-$325/pair

Two Carnelian I yellow pieces
a flat vase and a bulbous vase (chip to base), "Rv″ ink stamp to both, 6″ and 7 1/2″ tall.

$90-$110/pair

Three Carnelian I yellow vases
two squat (larger with fleck and restored chips at base, nicks and bruise to smaller), and an ovoid vase (restored chips at base), "Rv″ ink stamp to two; tallest: 10″.

$275-$325/set

Carnelian I yellow post-factory lamp base
with fittings, several small chips and lines, unmarked; pottery: 15 1/2″ tall.

$275-$325

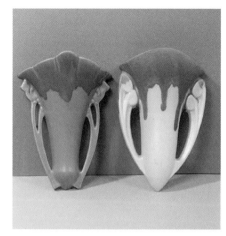

Two Carnelian I wall pockets
one covered in a dripping gray over pink glaze, and one in two shades of green; "Rv″ ink stamps, 8 1/2″ tall each.

$300-$400/pair

Carnelian II ewer
covered in a mottled pink glaze with purple drips from rim, repairs to handle, remnant of paper label, 15″ tall.

$550-$650

Carnelian II faceted center bowl
covered in a fine green, purple, and amber glaze, a few nicks to base, unmarked, 4″ by 15″.

$225-$275

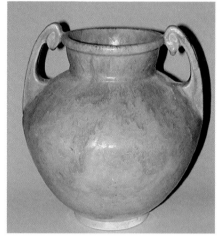

Carnelian II urn
in green and pink frothy matte glaze, unmarked, 9 1/2″ by 10″.

$400-$450

Two Carnelian II pieces
pink bud vase and blue and mottled green low bowl; some minute flecks and shallow scratches to each, paper label on one, 6″ tall and 6 1/4″ diameter.

$175-$225/pair

Carnelian II red bulbous vase
some grinding chips, unmarked, 7″ by 4 1/2″.

$350-$400

Carnelian II two-handled bulbous vase
in a green, purple, and rose frothy glaze, unmarked, 7″ by 5″.

$275-$325

Carnelian II spherical vase
mounted as a lamp base, with frothy blue and green matt glaze, post-factory drill hole, 8 1/2″ diameter.

$275-$325

Carnelian II spherical vase
covered in a fine frothy green, purple, and pink
glaze, glaze losses inside foot ring, unmarked,
8 1/2″ by 8 1/2″.

$1,400-$1,600

**Carnelian II squat two-handled
vase**
a few short tight lines to rim, repair to chip under
one handle, unmarked, 6 1/2″ by 9″.

$150-$200

Carnelian II two-handled vase
covered in a red and purple mottled glaze, burst
glaze bubble at handle, unmarked, 9″ by 8 1/4″.

$700-$800

Carnelian II urn
covered in a frothy teal and mauve glaze,
unmarked, 10″ by 6 1/2″.

$250-$300

**Carnelian II bulbous two-handled
vase**
covered in a fine green and turquoise mottled
glaze, a few light abrasions to body and fleck to
base, unmarked, 8 1/4″ by 8 1/2″.

$225-$275

**Carnelian II bulbous two-handled
vase**
covered in a fine pink dripping glaze, several
small nicks, stilt-pull chips, and a professional
restoration to chip at base, unmarked, 8″ by 8 3/4″.

$175-$225

Carnelian II bulbous vase
covered in a fine purple, green, and amber mottled
glaze, restoration to base, factory glaze line under
one handle, unmarked, 8 1/4″ by 9″.

$175-$225

Carnelian II classically shaped vase
covered in mottled mauve, brown, and ochre glaze,
unmarked, 9″ by 5 1/4″.

$350-$400

Carnelian II ovoid vase
with slightly flaring rim, covered in mottled mauve,
green, and ochre glaze, some burst bubbles,
unmarked, 7 1/2″ tall.

$225-$275

Carnelian II freestanding flower frog and candleholder

(63 - 3 1/2″) in dripping green, raspberry, and lavender glaze, "Rv" ink stamp, 3 7/8″ by 5 1/4″ by 4″.

$250-$350

Carnelian vase with squat base

and buttressed flaring neck, covered in a frothy pink and green glaze, a few very minor flakes to base, unmarked, 16 1/2″ by 11 1/4″.

$2,800-$3,200

Carnelian II vessel

covered in a deep green to rose glaze, minute nick to base, unmarked, 3 1/2″ by 6″.

$250-$300

Carnelian II vase

covered in fine pink, amber, and green frothy glazes, unmarked, 9 1/4″ by 5 1/2″.

$300-$350

Carnelian II ewer

(1311-10″), in dripping green, raspberry and lavender glaze, 10 3/8″ by 8″ by 5 1/2″.

$700-$800

Carnelian II wall pocket
in a frothy pink and ochre glaze, black paper label
and gift shop tag, 7 1/2″ by 5 3/4″.

$325-$375

Early Carnelian ovoid vase
unmarked, 11″ by 8 1/2″.

$200-$250

Early Carnelian vase
unmarked, 6″ tall.

$175-$225

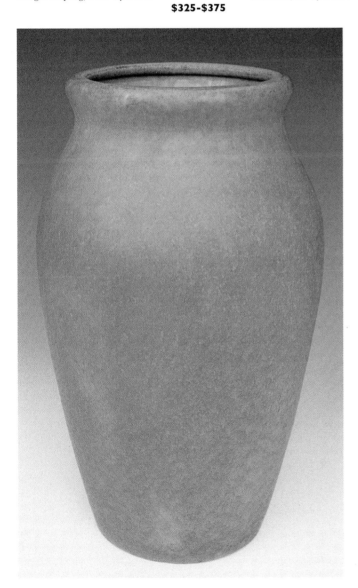

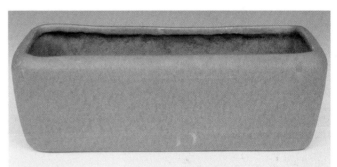

Early Carnelian planter or window box
unmarked, 8 3/4″ by 3″ by 3 1/2″.

$150-$200

Early Carnelian lamp base
unmarked, 12″ by 6 1/4″.

$300-$400

Early Carnelian vase
unmarked, 8″ tall.

$200-$250

Ceramic Design

Ceramic Design was a wide-ranging collection of styles and decoration, early 20th century, that borrowed freely from other Roseville lines in both shape and glaze, especially for urns, wall pockets, and planters. Most pieces are unmarked.

Ceramic Design creamware sugar bowl and creamer
enamel-decorated with forget-me-nots, hairline and chip to sugar bowl handle, unmarked, 3″ and 4 1/2″ tall.

$60–$80/pair

Ceramic Design planter
with spade-shaped flower and checkered design, covered in a matte green glaze, several repairs to feet, unmarked, 10 1/2″ by 12 1/2″.

$450–$550

Ceramic Design wall pocket
with restoration to tip, unmarked, 10″ tall.

$250–$300

Ceramic Design wall pocket
with five very small flat chips to back, and restoration to larger chip, unmarked, 18″ tall.

$1,100–$1,300

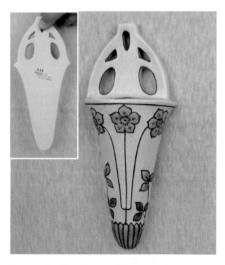

Ceramic Design wall pocket
(328), 10 3/4″ long.

$500–$600

Ceramic Design wall pocket
(330), unmarked, 11 3/4″ long.

$650–$750

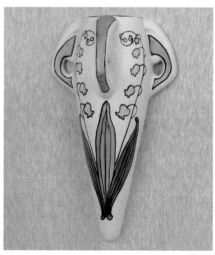

Ceramic Design wall pocket
(331), unmarked, 10 3/4″.

$650–$750

Cherry Blossom

Introduced in 1933, Cherry Blossom features a radiating pattern of contrasting stripes and textured ground overlaid with blossoming cherry branches. The brown and beige background is more common than the pink and green. Most pieces are unmarked or have a paper or foil label.

Cherry Blossom brown planter
unmarked, 4″ by 5″.

$200-$250

Cherry Blossom brown bulbous vase
unmarked, 5″ by 6 1/2″.

$300-$350

Cherry Blossom brown vase
unmarked, 12″ by 6 3/4″.

$800-$900

Cherry Blossom brown spherical vase
unmarked, 5 1/4″ by 5 1/2″.

$250-$300

Cherry Blossom brown spherical vase
with crisp mold, foil label, 8″ by 7 3/4″.

$650-$750

Cherry Blossom brown spherical vase
minor nick to one blossom, unmarked, 8 1/2" by 7 1/4".

$600-$700

Cherry Blossom brown ovoid vase
flea-bite to rim, unmarked, 10 1/4" by 6 1/4".

$600-$700

Cherry Blossom brown vase
with squat base, foil label, 8 1/4" by 5".

$450-$500

Cherry Blossom brown vessel
1/2" bruise to base, foil label, 5 1/2" by 7".

$250-$300

Cherry Blossom brown wall pocket
unmarked, 8" tall.

$950-$1,050

Cherry Blossom brown squat vessel
foil label, 4 1/4" by 5 1/2".

$200-$250

Cherry Blossom pink jardinière
with small clay pimples around flower and one short crazing line to rim, gold foil label, 4" by 5 1/2".

$350-$400

Cherry Blossom pink two-handled vase
unmarked, 10 1/2" by 6 1/2".

$1,300-$1,400

Chloron

Using many of the molds also found in Egypto and Matt Green, Chloron (circa 1908) is a dull green with raised motifs of flowers, leaves, figures, and faces. Some pieces have contrasting ivory panels. Pieces are often unmarked, but occasionally occur with an ink stamp.

Chloron tapering two-handled vessel
with scalloped rim, the body embossed with cherries, stamped "Chloron/T.R.P. Co.," 6 1/2" by 7".
$1,200-$1,300

Chloron wall sconce
with owl on ivory panel (339), 12 1/2" by 12 1/2".
$2,500-$3,000

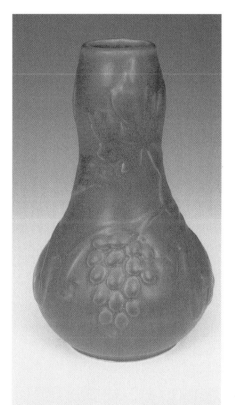

Chloron wall pocket
with face framed in grape clusters and leaves (346), 9 5/8" by 9".
$1,800-$2,200

Chloron vase
with raised grapes and leaf design, shape C22, stamped "Chloron/T.R.P. Co.," 8 1/4" tall.
$400-$450

Chloron low handled bowl
(shape 13), stamped "TRPCo. Chloron," 7 3/4" by 3 3/8".
$250-$300

Clemana

Sources vary on the introduction year of Clemana, ranging from 1934 to 1936. The design features stylized white flowers and green leaves on a striated pattern similar to long narrow thorns. Background colors are blue, brown, and green. Pieces have an impressed mark.

A pair of Clemana bowls
(281-5˝):one brown with chip repair to rim and one blue with small chip to rim, impressed marks.

$150-$200/pair

Clemana blue chalice
(122-7˝), impressed mark.

$350-$400

Two Clemana blue vases
(752-7˝) and (749-6˝) with minute stilt-pull, impressed mark.

$450-$500/pair

Clemana blue flaring urn
(759-14˝), restoration to chip on one handle and rim and several around base, impressed mark.
$550-$650

Two Clemana brown bulbous vases
751-7˝ with restoration to chips at rim and base, and 752-7˝, impressed marks.
$275-$300/pair

Two Clemana brown vessels
one bulbous (754-8˝) with two chips to bottom, and one footed (122-7˝), impressed marks.
$375-$400/pair

Two Clemana green vases
752-7″ with restoration to chips at rim and base, and 750-6″, impressed marks.
$300-$350/pair

Clemana green flaring vessel
(753-8″), minor fleck to rim, impressed mark.
$275-$300

Clemana green spherical vase
(754-8″), restoration to one handle, impressed mark.
$175-$225

Clematis

Introduced in 1944, Clematis features broad blossoms of six or seven petals and a trailing ivy vine (that bears little or no resemblance to real clematis leaves) on a textured background of blue, brown, or green. Pieces have raised marks.

Clematis blue low handled bowl
(459-10″), 13 3/4″ by 11 1/2″ by 4″.
$300-$350

Clematis blue cookie jar
(3-8″), two large chips to base, flecks inside lid, and chip to one flower, raised mark.
$110-$140

Clematis blue tea set
comprised of a teapot
(5), creamer (5-C) with small chip at base, and sugar bowl (5-S) in as-is condition (chips and cracks), raised marks.
$125-$175

Two Clematis blue cornucopia vases
(141-8″): drilled hole to base of one and three chips to base of the other, raised marks.
$35-$50/pair

Clematis blue wall pocket
unmarked, 8 1/8″ by 5 3/4″ by 2 5/8″.

$325-$375

Three Clematis pieces
blue basket (387-7″) with filled-in chip to base, blue fan vase (193-6″), and green bulbous vase (188-6″), all marked.

$150-$200/set

Three Clematis brown pieces
a pair of double bud vases (194-5″) with crack and nick to one, and a large bowl (461-14″), all marked.

$175-$225/set

Five Clematis brown pieces
double bud vase (194-5″) with nick and small repair, bud vase (187-7″) with repaired rim, bulbous vase (102-6″), another bulbous vase (103-6″) with repaired handle, and triple vase (192-5″) with small chip to base, all marked.

$175-$225/set

Clematis brown cookie jar
(3-8˝), bruise and small nicks to lid, and bruises and nicks to jar, marked.

$200-$250

Three Clematis brown pieces
triple bud vase/flower frog (50) with spider cracks, rectangular planter (391-8˝) with nick to handle, and console bowl (458-10˝) with reglued chips, all marked.

$110-$140/set

Three Clematis brown vases
(190-6˝, 105-7˝, 192-5˝): restoration to base of 7˝, chip to 5˝, all marked.

$110-$140/set

Clematis brown candleholder
(1159-4 1/2˝), raised mark, 4 3/4˝ by 4˝.

$70-$80

Clematis brown ewer vase
(16-6˝), 6˝ by 6 1/2˝ by 6 1/4˝.

$175-$225

Clematis brown bulbous vase
(103-6˝), raised mark, 6 1/4˝ by 5˝ by 4 1/2˝.

$150-$200

Two Clematis brown pieces
bulbous vase (107-8″) and ewer (17-10″), raised marks.

$175-$225/pair

Three Clematis green pieces
small basket (387-7″) with repair to large portion of handle and base, larger basket (389-10″) with fleck and bruise to base, and urn (188-6″), raised marks.

$175-$225/set

Clematis green tea set
(5) with some pockmarks to base and several small chips under foot ring of teapot, burst bubble to spout, and minor glaze miss to base of creamer, raised marks; teapot: 7 3/4″ by 11″.

$200-$250/set

Clematis green cookie jar
(3-8″), raised mark, 9″ by 10 1/4″.

$800-$900

Clematis green bud vase
(192-5″), 5 1/8″ by 6″ by 3 5/8″.

$150-$200

Clematis green fan/cornucopia vase
(193-6″), raised mark, 6 1/4″ by 6 1/4″ by 3 5/8″.

$125-$150

Clematis green bulbous vase
(107-8″), raised mark, 8 1/4″ by 6 3/4″ by 6 1/2″.

$175-$200

Columbine

Introduced in 1941, Columbine has a large bloom on tall slender stems with trailing leaves and three-leaf clusters. Background colors are blue, brown to green, and pink to green. Pieces have raised marks.

Columbine blue basket
(368-12″), raised mark.

$350-$450

Pair of Columbine blue bookend planters
(8), raised marks, 5 1/4″ by 5″ by 5″.

$200-$250/pair

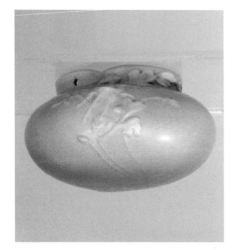

Columbine blue hanging basket
2″ bruise to rim, burst bubble to one hole, unmarked, 4 3/4″ by 8″.

$110-$140

Three Columbine ewers
(18-7″):one pink with a few small chips under foot ring, one brown, and one blue, raised marks.

$325-$375/set

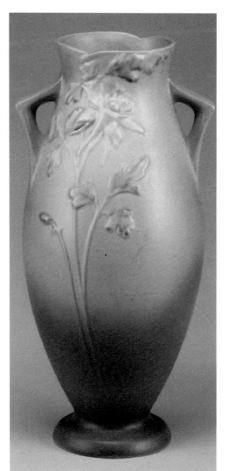

Columbine blue tall bulbous vase
(27-16″), raised mark.

$425-$475

Three Columbine blue pieces
squat vase (399-4″) and a pair of candlesticks (1145-2 1/2″), all marked.

$150-$200/set

Three Columbine pieces
two planters, one blue (655-3″) and one pink (399-4″), and a pink vase (16-7″), chips to each, one reglued, all marked.

$150-$200/set

Four Columbine pieces
brown urn (151-8˝) and three bulbous vases (12-4˝), two brown and one pink (chip to rim), all marked.

$275-$325/set

Two Columbine vases
one brown (150-6˝) with crisp mold and 1/4˝ glaze bubble to flower, and one blue (22-9˝), raised marks.

$225-$275/pair

Columbine brown classically shaped vase
(23-10˝), good mold and color, raised mark.

$200-$250

Pair of Columbine brown planter bookends
(8), raised marks, 5 1/4˝ by 5˝ by 5˝.

$200-$250/pair

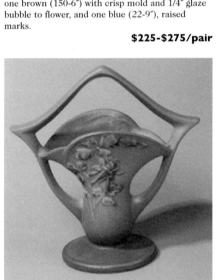

Columbine brown basket
(365-7˝), raised mark.

$225-$275

Columbine pink basket
(367-10˝), pinhead size fleck on one stem, raised mark.

$175-$225

Columbine pink candlesticks
(1145-2 1/2˝), both marked.

$90-$110/pair

Columbine pink vase
(21-9˝), raised mark, 9 1/4˝ by 6 3/8˝ by 5 3/4˝.

$225-$275

Columbine pink vase
(24-10″), raised mark, 10 3/8″ by 7 3/4″ by 6″.

$200-$250

Columbine squat vessel
(655-3″), 3″ by 5 1/4″.

$200-$250

Corinthian

A successor to Donatello, Corinthian (circa 1923) features a radiating fluted design in green and ivory with a band of entwined grape vines and fruit below a modified egg-and-dart border. Pieces are unmarked or with an "Rv" ink stamp.

Corinthian hanging basket
with small nick to hanging holes, unmarked, 8 3/4″ wide.

$150-$200

Corinthian wall pocket
"Rv" ink stamp, 9 1/4″ tall.

$200-$225

Corinthian wall pocket
"Rv" ink mark, 9 1/2″ tall.

$250-$300

Cosmos

Introduced in 1939, Cosmos features clusters of large blossoms on a contrasting irregular band, set against a textured background of blue, brown, or green. There is a mix of raised and impressed marks, or foil labels.

Cosmos blue spherical basket
(357-10″) with two chips to petals and chip to handle, raised mark.

$175-$225

Cosmos blue flowerpot with under plate
(650-5″), soft mold, raised mark.

$175-$225

Three Cosmos bulbous planters
green and brown (649-3″), and blue (649-4″), raised marks.

$250-$300/set

Two Cosmos blue pieces
double bud vase (133-4 1/2″) with some grinding chips to base, and rectangular planter (381-9″) with good mold, raised marks.

$300-$350/pair

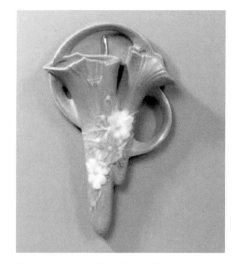

Cosmos blue double wall pocket
(1266-6″), silver foil label.

$500-$600

Cosmos blue floor vase
with scalloped, flaring rim (958-18″), very good mold and color, minute fleck to rim, possibly in firing, raised mark.

$650-$750

Cosmos blue two-handled vase
(948-7″), impressed mark.

$175-$225

Two Cosmos footed urns
(135-8″): one blue (with foil label) and one brown, one has restoration to cracked foot and fleck to petal, raised marks.

$200-$250/pair

Two Cosmos ewers
(957-15″), one brown with some minor flakes to high points and one green with reglued spout and flakes to high points, impressed marks.

$400-$450/pair

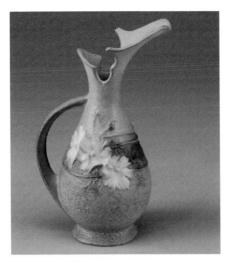

Cosmos brown ewer
(955-10″), impressed mark.

$300-$350

Cosmos brown footed basket planter
(357-10″), raised mark.

$200-$250

Cosmos brown urn
(956-12″), restoration to rim chip, raised mark.

$225-$275

Cosmos green basket
(358-12″) with restoration to crack at rim, raised mark.

$110-$140

Cosmos green footed basket planter
(358-12″), soft mold, raised mark.

$400-$450

Two Cosmos green pieces
flaring vase (947-6″) and squat vessel (375-4″) with several small nicks to decoration and base, raised marks.

$175-$225/pair

Cosmos green vase
with buttressed base, unmarked, 18 1/2″ by 8 1/2″ by 9 1/4″.

$1,000-$1,200

Creamwares

The Roseville creamwares, most
of which date from 1910 to 1920,
included the Juvenile line, novelty steins,
fraternal items, smoker sets, shaving
mugs, and even pin boxes. They were
rarely marked.

Creamware advertising matchbook holder
for Fatima Turkish
cigarettes, wear to
gilding, small chips
under foot ring,
unmarked, 3 1/2″ by 6″.
$80-$90

Eight assorted transfer-printed pieces
"F.O.E." tankard
and two mugs;
two "Should Auld
Acquaintance..."
mugs; Quaker
Children small
dish; Kosair
commemorative
mug, 1934; and
Knights of Pythias
pipe stand; some
minor chips, heights
range from 12″ to
2 1/2″.
$350-$400/set

"Good Night" candleholder
unmarked, 6 1/2″ by 4 1/2″ by
6″(with handle, not shown).
$500-$600

Three Creamware mugs
decorated with an Indian,
and the emblems of the
Fraternal Order of the
Elks and Eagles, between
4 1/2″ and 5″ tall.
$200-$250/each

Cremo

The Cremo line is among the rarest Roseville patterns, and consequently among the most expensive. The undulating forms introduced about 1912 have tiny stylized flowers and stems draped on glossy glazed vessels with colors that blend from dusty pink at the top to yellow, streaked green, and dark green. They are unmarked.

Cremo vase
shape No. 11, 7 3/4″ tall.

$1,400-$1,500

Cremona

Introduced in 1927, Cremona features a diffuse or mottled pastel background of celadon green (sometimes fading to pale yellow or gray accents) or dusty pink (pale blue is rare), with stylized flowers and leaves in various simple arrangements. Pieces are unmarked or have foil labels.

Cremona green baluster vase
unmarked, 12 1/4″ tall.

$325-$375

Cremona green pillow vase
minor nick to rim and dark crazing line to foot, unmarked, 6″ by 6 1/2″.

$45-$55

Cremona green vase
with buttressed handles near rim, decorated with small roses and leaves, unmarked, 8 1/4″ by 3 3/4″.

$225-$275

Cremona green four-sided vase
1/4″ glaze inconsistency under rim, unmarked, 10 1/4″ by 4″.

$250-$300

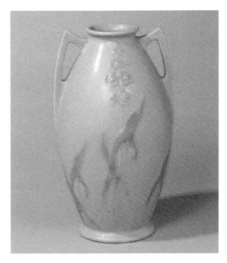

Cremona green bulbous vase
with two handles, unmarked, 10 1/4″ by 6″.
$250-$300

Cremona pink low bowl and flower frog
the bowl with pumpkins around its edges, unmarked, 2 3/4″ by 8 1/2″ diameter; frog, 1 1/2″ by 3 3/4″ diameter.
$225-$275

Cremona pink flaring vase
with two buttressed handles at rim, unmarked, 12″ by 6″.
$250-$300

Cremona flaring vase
in pink and green glazes, unmarked, 8″ by 5 1/2″.
$150-$175

Cremona pink four-sided vase
with blue blossoms, small chips at base (show very slightly on side) and 1″ chip to rim, unmarked, 10″ by 4″.
$150-$200

Cremona pink ovoid vase
with two handles, small glaze bubbles throughout, silver foil label, 10″ by 6″.
$175-$225

Cremona pink shouldered vase
with flaring rim, unmarked, 10″ by 6″.
$175-$225

Cremona pink vase
with lavender freesia, burst bubbles to rim, unmarked, 12 1/4″ by 4″.
$175-$225

Crocus

Introduced about 1912, Crocus features stylized flowers and line decoration regularly spaced around the vessels using the squeeze-bag technique. Pieces are unmarked or have artist initials.

Crocus green jardinière
with four buttressed handles, touched-up 2 1/2″ bruise to rim, scratches, and several pock marks, unmarked, 9″ by 12″.

$650-$750

Crocus bulbous vase
restoration to glaze chips at base, fleck to rim, 9 3/4″ by 4″.

$300-$350

Courtesy Adamstown Antique Gallery

Crocus bulbous vase
with stepped rim, squeeze-bag decorated in blue, yellow, and green, unmarked, 6″ tall.

$850-$950

Crocus green vase
with flaring rim, squeeze-bag decorated in blue, yellow, and green, restoration to chips at base, small flakes to rim, some touched-up, signed "RH," 9″ by 4″.

$300-$350

Two Crocus vases
both with stylized floral motifs, right: bottle vase, unmarked, 6 7/8″ tall, $450-$550; left, three-sided vase, unmarked, 8 1/8″ tall.

$650-$750

Two Crocus vases and an Aztec oil lamp
all with stylized floral motifs, right: cylindrical, unmarked, 9 3/4″ tall, $600-$700; oil lamp, unmarked, 11″ tall,

$750-$850;

left, bottle form, unmarked, 9 1/4″ tall.

$550-$650

Crystalis

Introduced about 1905 and part of the Rozane Wares, Crystalis is usually found in a speckled gold and ivory glaze, and pieces often have arching or angular buttressed supports. Pieces are unmarked or have a paper Rozane Ware label.

Crystalis ring-handle vase
in an Egypto shape (E 58) with a mottled salmon and gold glaze, some restoration, with "Rozane Ware/Egypto" wafer, 14 7/8″ tall.

$1,500-$1,800

Crystalis squat vessel
with buttressed supports around neck, 4″ by 6 1/4″.

$1,800-$1,900

Dahlrose

Dating from the 1920s, Dahlrose features large daisy-like blossoms with brown centers on a textured body that changes from muddy green to terra cotta brown. Pieces are unmarked or have paper labels.

Two Dahlrose pieces
center bowl and ovoid vase; small nick inside rim, flat chip to base of bowl; vase: 8″ tall.

$125-$175/pair

Dahlrose oval center bowl
reglued flat chip to rim, unmarked, 4 1/2″ by 10 1/4″.

$110-$140

Dahlrose console set
consisting of a small oval center bowl and a pair of candlesticks, minute fleck to handle of one candlestick, unmarked; bowl: 10 1/2″ diameter; candlesticks: 3 1/2″ tall.

$250-$350/set

Dahlrose flower pot
with under plate, short firing line to rim of pot and short tight line to rim of under plate, unmarked, 5 1/2″ by 6″.

$200-$250

Dahlrose jardinière
1/2″ chip to base, unmarked, 8″ by 11″.

$225-$275

Dahlrose jardinière and pedestal
several small chips and lines, unmarked; jardinière: 8 1/4″ tall; pedestal: 16 1/2″ tall.

$450-$500

Two Dahlrose pieces
small jardinière (two minor repaired chips to base) and a planter (tight cracks and repaired rim), both unmarked; taller: 4 1/4″.

$125-$175/pair

Two Dahlrose pieces

four-sided vase with flaring rim (restored chips at rim) and flat vase with strong mold (some small chips at base and tight line to rim), unmarked, 6" and 6 1/4" tall.

$325-$375/pair

Three Dahlrose pieces

hanging basket with crisp mold (chip, repair, line), ovoid vase (large repaired chip to base), and spherical vase, unmarked; tallest: 6".

$225-$275/set

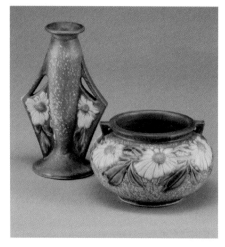

Three Dahlrose pieces

single and double bud vase, and flat vase (touched-up), paper label; tallest: 7".

$275-$325/set

Two Dahlrose pieces

bud vase and bulbous planter, black paper labels, 8 1/4" tall and 4 1/2" by 6 3/4".

$350-$400/pair

Two Dahlrose pieces

triple bud vase with strong mold and bulbous vase, black paper label to one, 6 1/4" and 8 1/2" tall.

$275-$325/pair

Two Dahlrose pieces

ovoid planter and vase (restoration to two chips at foot), unmarked; planter: 4 1/2" by 10 1/2"; vase: 6 1/2" tall.

$175-$225/pair

Two Dahlrose pieces

spherical vase (painted overglaze chip at base and two flecks) and ovoid vase (chip to base), 4 1/4" by 4 1/2" and 6 1/4" by 3 1/4".

$250-$300/pair

Dahlrose rectangular planter

some minor nicks, excellent condition overall, unmarked, 6 1/4" by 12".

$300-$350

Dahlrose planter
with small nick to leaf, 7 1/4″ by 10″.
$110-$140

Dahlrose rectangular planter
good mold, unmarked, rare in this size, 6 1/4″ by 13″.
$500-$600

Dahlrose bud vase
unmarked, 3 1/8″ by 6″.
$175-$225

Dahlrose double bud vase
unmarked, 7 1/2″ by 6 1/4″ by 2 1/4″.
$275-$325

Dahlrose triple bud vase
black paper label, 6 1/2″ tall.
$125-$175

Two Dahlrose bud vases
one double; minor chip inside foot ring on double, one has foil label, 6 1/4″ by 7 1/2″ and 7 1/4″ by 5 1/2″.
$350-$400/pair

Dahlrose bulbous vase
touch-up to base, small bruise to one handle, unmarked, 8″ by 7″.
$125-$175

Two Dahlrose pieces
urn with buttressed handles (crack to one handle, overpainted small chips at rim) and bulbous vase, unmarked, 10″ by 7 1/4″ and 6 1/4″ by 4 1/4″.
$275-$325/pair

Dahlrose footed urn
with flaring rim, black paper label, 12 1/4″ by 9″.
$450-$550

Dahlrose bulbous vase
some glaze inconsistency to flowers, unmarked, 10″ tall.
$200-$250

Dahlrose bulbous vase
with strong mold, unmarked, 10″ by 9″.
$1,000-$1,200

Dahlrose shouldered vessel
with two short handles, shallow firing line to body, unmarked, 6 1/4″ by 8″.
$150-$175

Two Dahlrose pieces
squat vessel and an oval planter, latter has soft mold and minute fleck to one handle, unmarked, 4 1/2″ by 6 1/2″ and 4 1/2″ by 10 1/2″.
$225-$275/pair

Dahlrose bulbous vessel
with flaring rim, excellent mold and color, black paper label, 9 1/4″ by 7″.
$800-$900

Two Dahlrose vases
one tapering four-sided with good mold and minor chip inside foot ring, and bud vase with buttressed handles, unmarked, 6 1/4″ by 3 1/2″ and 8 1/4″ by 5″.
$450-$550/pair

Dahlrose wall pocket
chip to tip, 10 1/4″ tall.
$125-$175

Dawn

Introduced in 1937, the art deco-influenced Dawn has a stark, spidery leaf decoration on soft green, pink, or yellow backgrounds, and most pieces have footed or buttressed bases. Examples have an impressed mark or foil label.

Dawn green spherical jardinière
(316-6″), minor fleck to corner of one handle, another to corner of base, foil label and impressed mark.

$250-$300

Dawn green cylindrical vase
restoration to rim chip, illegible mark, 11 1/4″ by 7 1/2″.

$400-$450

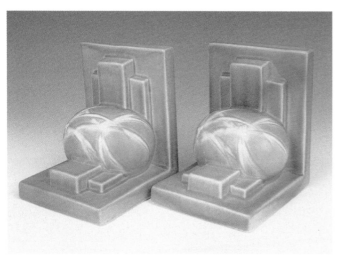

Pair of Dawn green bookends
(4), impressed mark, 5 1/4″ by 4 1/4″ by 4 1/2″.
$450-$500/pair

Pair of Dawn pink bookends
(4), impressed mark, 5 1/4″ by 4 1/4″ by 4 1/2″
$450-$550/pair

Two Dawn pink vases
(826-6″ and 829-8″), impressed marks.
$300-$350/pair

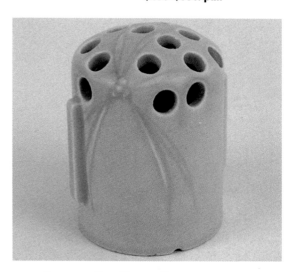

Dawn yellow flower frog
(31-3x4″), impressed mark.
$150-$175

Dealer's Signs

Easily damaged, dealer's signs command a premium in mint condition. Most date from the second quarter of the 20th century and come in a range of glaze colors. New signs are being made, so beware of reproductions.

Dealer's sign
in blue and yellow glazes, glaze miss to top of "L," 5″ by 8″.

$2,100-$2,300

Dealer's sign
with light pink letters on a deep rose matte ground, restoration to several chips, 6 1/4″ long.

$800-$900

Dealer's sign
in green, 4 1/4″ by 9 1/2″.

$2,600-$2,800

Dealer's sign
in pink, 2 1/4″ by 6 1/4″.

$1,200-$1,400

Dealer's sign
in blue, 4″ by 9 3/8″.

$2,800-$3,000

Dealer's sign
1 1/2″ by 5 1/2″.

$1,400-$1,500

Dealer's sign
4 5/8″ by 7 1/2″.

$2,500-$2,800

Decorated Matt

The line called Decorated Matt evolved from other Roseville patterns popular between 1905 and 1910, and reflects influences of the art nouveau and arts & crafts movements. Soft colors of dusty blue and tan for backgrounds are contrasted with bold geometric and stylized forms from nature in cream, yellow, navy, and terra cotta. These pieces are usually unmarked, but may include an artist's signature.

Decorated Matt jardinière in gray-blue with geometric design along rim in cream, yellow, and brown, unmarked, 6 1/4″ tall.
$1,500-$1,800

Della Robbia

Designed by Frederick H. Rhead about 1905 as part of the Rozane Wares, and named for a 15th century Florentine family of sculptors and ceramists famous for their enameled terracotta or faience, the Della Robbia group is the most complex and diverse collection of Roseville pieces, as well as the rarest. Borrowing freely from centuries of decorative themes—stretching from ancient Greece to the American Arts & Crafts movement—Della Robbia is the Holy Grail of Roseville collectors. A Della Robbia vase holds the world auction record for a piece of Roseville, selling for $38,850 in 1999.

Della Robbia teapot excised with hearts, cups and saucers, and Japanese fans, in brown and celadon, small nicks to lid, 1″ clay burst to rim of pot and 1/2″ chip to base, Rozane Ware wafer, 9″ by 8″
$1,100-$1,200.

Della Robbia teapot its lid with the inscription "Polly put the kettle on/we'll all have tea/Sukie take it off again/it's all boiled away"; the body with two excised panels, each depicting a woman in a kitchen holding a kettle, in beige and brown, restoration to lid, several nicks and cracks to base, restoration to spout, Rozane Ware wafer, 5 3/4″ by 7 1/2″.
$500-$600

Della Robbia vase unusual example with deeply carved and cut-back floral design, whiplash stems and leaves in a multitoned green glaze, signed with wafer mark, artist signed, 14″ tall, two minor flakes.
$5,000-$6,000

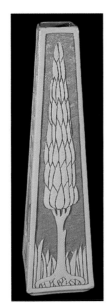

Della Robbia vase obelisk form with stylized trees set on a tan background, wafer mark, 10 1/2″ by 2 3/4″.
$4,500-$5,000

Della Robbia vase cylindrical with stylized flowers on a brown background, 10″ by 5″, wafer mark and incised artist initials.
$5,000-$6,000

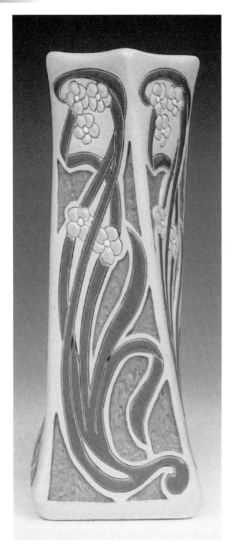

Della Robbia vase
twisted four-sided form with tiny lavender blossoms and sinuous dark green leaves, marked twice with an inscribed "E," 9 3/4" tall.

$2,500-$2,800

Della Robbia oil lamp
shape D-6, in sage and cream with large stylized leaves and blossoms, Rozane Ware wafer, 11 1/8" tall.

$2,000-$2,200

Della Robbia pillow vase
shape No. 5, with a large stylized blossom in sage and dark green, Rozane Ware wafer, 7 3/8" tall.

$2,200-$2,400

Della Robbia spherical vase
shape No. 10, with five bands of daisies, Rozane Ware wafer, 8" tall.

$2,800-$3,000

Dogwood I and II

There are two distinct Dogwood patterns: textured (called Dogwood I, circa 1916) and smooth (called Dogwood II, mid-1920s). The earlier version has subtler shades and an olive-colored background; pieces were unmarked or ink stamped. The later pattern is a more intense green shot with brown, and the branches are nearly all black; pieces were seldom marked.

Dogwood I rectangular planter
complete with original liner, strong mold, good glazing, minor fleck to body, unmarked, 6 1/4" by 11 1/2".

$150-$175

Two Dogwood I vessels
one squat (good mold, small glaze flake to petal) and one bulbous (several small flakes to petals), both have "Rv" ink stamps, 4″ by 7″ and 8 1/4″ by 6 1/2″.

$150-$200/pair

Two wall pockets
Dogwood I and double Dogwood II (small flake to tip), first one has "Rv" ink stamp, the other is unmarked, 9″ by 5″ and 8 1/4″ by 6 1/2″.

$400-$500/pair

Dogwood I bulbous urn
with good mold, crack to one handle, small pockmark to rim, "Rv" ink stamp, 12″ by 7 1/2″.

$800-$1,000

Dogwood II jardinière
restoration to rim chip and several glaze chips (some restored) to petals, unmarked, 8 1/2″ by 10″.

$175-$200

Three Dogwood II pieces
basket vase, bud vase (soft mold, several small burst chips underneath), and bowl; 9″ by 4 1/2″, 9″ by 3 1/2″, and 2 3/4″ by 6 1/4″.

$300-$400/set

Dogwood II almond-shaped planter
complete with original liner, good mold and glazing, 1″ bruise to rim of planter, minor bruise to base, and several chips to liner, illegible stamp mark, rare, 6″ by 11 1/4″.

$900-$1,100

Donatella

With a strong art nouveau influence, Donatella (circa 1912) was also part of the creamwares and featured geometric, cameo, figural, and floral motifs. These pieces are unmarked. The angular handles and long, narrow spots are easily damaged, so beware of restorations.

Donatella coffeepot and creamer
(style E) decorated with a stylized floral motif; teapot 6 1/2″ tall.
$600-$700/pair

Donatello

Also designed by Frederick Rhead, Donatello (circa 1915) had lighter green and beige fluting than Corinthian. A frieze of cherubs encircled the vessels with a brown background. Pieces were usually unmarked, or had an "Rv″ ink stamp or paper label.

Two Donatello pieces
small basket and a wall pocket; bruise, line, and some nicks to rim of basket, chip to rear side of hanging hole; Donatello stamp mark to one, "Rv″ ink stamp to other; 8″ and 10 1/2″ tall.
$175-$225/pair

Pair of Donatello baskets with arched handles
soft mold, one has short underglaze line to rim (does not go through) and minute fleck to one rib, unmarked, 9 1/4″ by 6 1/4″ each.
$450-$500/pair

Donatello bowl
"R″ stamped in ink on the bottom, 6 1/4″ by 2 5/8″.
$70-$90

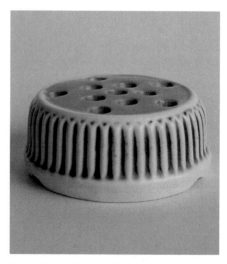

Donatello flower frog
unmarked, 3 1/2″ by 1 5/8″.
$120-$140

Donatello cuspidor or spittoon
unmarked, significant crazing to interior, 7 1/2″ by 5 3/8″.
$225-$250

Donatello jardinière
ink stamp (575-8″), rim chip, 7 1/2″ by 10″.
$200-$250

Donatello jardinière and pedestal
chip repair inside rim of jardinière, "Rv" ink stamp
to pedestal; pedestal: 18″ by 11 1/2″; jardinière: 9″
by 11″.
$180-$220

**Donatello trial glaze jardinière and
pedestal set**
with band of winged cherubs in the forest, lines to
interior and one to base of jardinière, glaze flake
to base of pedestal, unmarked, jardinière: 10″ tall;
pedestal: 18″ tall.
$650-$750

Donatello bud vase
(116-6″), 6 1/8″ by 2 3/8″.
$180-$220

Two Donatello pieces
pitcher (several flecks) and an unusual chamberstick (1/4″ chip to base), unmarked; pitcher: 6 1/4″ tall.

$125-$175/pair

Donatello "gate" or double bud vase
black paper label, 7 3/4″ by 4 3/8″ by 2″.

$125-$150

Donatello bulbous vase
several flat chips to base, unmarked, 10 1/4″ tall.

$300-$350

Pair of Donatello flaring vases
both with some nicks to rim, unmarked, 8″ by 3 3/4″ each.

$150-$200/pair

Donatello footed vase
unmarked, 10″ by 4 1/2″.

$110-$140

Donatello vase
normal abrasion and small bruise to base, unmarked, 9 1/2″ by 5 1/2″.

$80-$100

Dutch

Part of the creamware line, circa 1915, the Dutch transfer decoration was found on cups, pitchers, teapots, and other utilitarian wares. Pieces were unmarked.

Tall Dutch pitcher
(lemonade?), with transfer decoration, 11″ tall, unmarked.

$250-$350

Assorted Dutch mugs
with transfer decorations, each between 4″ and 5″ tall, unmarked.

$80-$120 each, depending on condition.

E

Earlam

Introduced in 1930, Earlam combines soft glaze colors that blurred from tan to pink and blue to gray, with pale greens and light browns. The shapes are deceptively simple, echoing Chinese Neolithic pottery. Pieces are unmarked or have paper/foil labels.

Earlam blue strawberry jar or planter
unmarked, 8″ by 6 1/2″.

$800-$900

Pair of Earlam green chambersticks
black paper labels, 4″ by 7″.

$400-$500

Earlam vase
shape 517, with trial glaze semigloss decoration of hand-painted leaves on a peach ground, marked "trial no. 38″ under the base, 5 1/2″.

$1,100

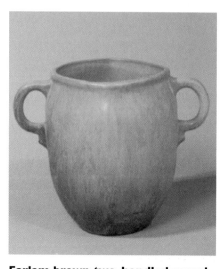

Earlam brown two-handled vessel
with four-sided rim, unmarked, 6 1/4″ by 7 1/2″.

$400-$450

Earlam green strawberry jar
unmarked, 8″ by 6 1/2″.

$800-$900

Earlam green four-sided planter
with arched rim, unmarked, 5 1/4″ by 10 1/4″ by
2 1/2″.

$225-$275

Earlam ginger jar
V-shaped bruise to the inner part of the lid, gold
foil label, 10 3/4″ by 6″.

$250-$300

Two Earlam vessels
one pink and one green, pink piece has a 2″
hairline, unmarked, 5″ by 5 1/4″, and 4 1/4″ by
5 3/4″.

$175-$225/pair

Earlam two-handled vase
with four-sided rim, in pink and blue, unmarked,
6″ by 8″.

$350-$400

Five Earlam pieces
two pairs of candlesticks and a flower frog, flower frog has an underglaze chip to base, black paper labels to
three; candlesticks: 4 1/4″ and 2 1/2″ tall.

$375-$425/set

Earlam wall pocket
unmarked, 6 1/2″ tall.

$750-$850

Early Wares

These pieces, usually pitchers and cuspidors, date from before 1920 and were part of the utility line. The raised and hand-painted images have a naïve folk art appeal and include animals, flowers, figures, and landscapes. None are marked.

Early cuspidor
with tulips in an indigo glossy glaze with gilded details, 1/4″ chip to rim, abrasion to base, unmarked, 5 1/2″ by 8″.

0-$60

Early pitcher
with Dutch figures (called "No. 2 Holland"), 9 1/4″ tall.

$200-$250

Set of four early mugs
with a Dutch boy on one side and a Dutch girl on the other, 4″ tall.

$60-$80/set

Early pitcher
with farm landscape, repair, and line to spout, unmarked, 7 1/2″ by 8 3/4″.

$60-$80

Two early pitchers
with landscapes in as-is condition (chips, cracks, lines, touch-ups), unmarked, 7 1/2″ tall each.

$125-$175/pair

Two early pitchers
one Iris and one with Dutchman (lines at rim possibly from firing, several glaze bursts), unmarked, 8 1/2″ and 9″ tall.

$175-$225/pair

Two early pitchers
one with cow (a few short lines), the other with tulip (small chip to spout, hairline near handle), unmarked, 7 1/2″ tall each.

$250-$300/pair

Early pitchers
floral, unmarked, 9 1/2″ tall,

$250-$300

cow, unmarked, 7 1/2″ tall.

$200-$250

Early pitcher
in blended glaze, unmarked, 7 1/2″ tall.

$200-$250

Early pitcher known as "The Boy″
(two views), unmarked, 7 1/2″ tall, seen in as-found condition, if perfect.

$400-$500

Egypto

Part of the Rozane Wares, Egypto (circa 1905) has less to do with Egypt and more to do with the American Arts & Crafts movement, with its soft green glaze and naturalistic forms. Sometimes unmarked, many pieces have a "Rozane Ware/Egypto″ stamp on an applied wafer.

Egypto pitcher
in oil lamp form, unmarked, 5″ by 6″.

$550-$650

Egypto factory lamp
base embossed with three Indian men on
elephants, three factory drill holes, complete
with a converted oil font, small chip and some
unevenness to base, marked with Rozane Ware/
Egypto wafer; 10 1/4″ by 9″ without font.
$2,800-$3,200

Egypto inkwell and cover
fine and rare, of classical design, with Caesar
medallion on lid, a wreath of laurels, columns, and
classical motifs around drum base, all covered in
a fine curdled matte green glaze, very tight line
to rim, probably from firing, excellent overall
condition, Egypto wafer, 3 3/4″ by 5″.
$600-$700

Egypto oil lamp
on tall tapering foot, embossed with lotus plants,
hairlines to base, Egypto wafer, 9 1/2″ by 9″.
$650-$750

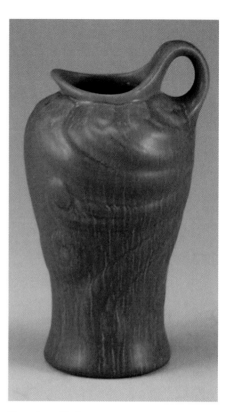

Egypto pitcher
embossed with waves under a feathered matte
green glaze, unmarked, 7 1/2″ tall.
$500-$600

Egypto corseted tankard
typical glaze pulling at base with minor grinding
chips, unmarked, 10 1/2″ by 5″.
$750-$850

Egypto urn
embossed with pattern around neck, 1/2″ chip to
handle, Egypto wafer, 8 1/2″ by 6 1/4″.
$375-$425

Egypto bud vase
grinding chips, 5 1/2″ by 2 1/2″.
$450-$500

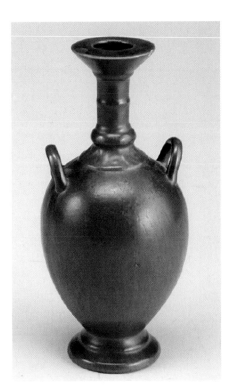

Egypto urn
with bulbous body and flaring neck, covered in a
fine rich green semi-matte glaze, chip to rim and
large stilt-pull chip to base, Rozane wafer, 9 3/4″
by 4 1/2″.

$275-$325

Egypto small pitcher
with raised geometric band around shoulder, small
flat nick to base, Egypto wafer, 3 1/4″ tall.

$175-$225

Egypto vase
embossed with lotus leaves and blossoms, all
covered in a smooth vellum medium-green matte
glaze, Egypto wafer, 8 1/2″ by 8″.

$3,700-$3,800

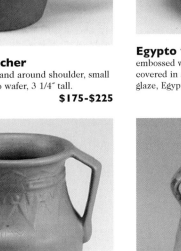

Egypto two-handled vase
embossed with band of diamonds, restoration to
chip on handle, Egypto wafer, 6 1/2″ by 6 1/2″.

$225-$275

Egypto two-handled vessel
fleck at base, burst bubbles throughout, unmarked,
5 1/2″ by 5 1/4″.

$300-$350

Egypto tall tapering vase
its neck embossed with a band of diamonds,
covered in a frothy matte green glaze, Rozane
wafer, 12 1/2″ by 4 1/4″.

$1,700-$1,900

Egypto vessel
with scalloped rim and embossed broad leaves to
body, unmarked, 5 1/4″ by 5″.

$400-$450

Egypto squat two-handled vessel
embossed with cherries and leaves, Egypto wafer, 5
1/2″ by 7 1/2″.

$600-$700

Elsie

The Elsie juvenile ware set of bowl, cup, and plate was made in the late 1940s.

Borden Milk Company three-piece child's breakfast set commemorating Elsie the Cow and Beauregard the Bull, consisting of a plate (7 1/2″ diameter), bowl (5 1/2″ diameter) and mug (2 1/2″ diameter), all covered in a glossy pumpkin glaze, minor wear to surface decoration on plate and bowl, raised marks.

$750-$850

Experimentals, Trial Glazes

Experimental pieces sometimes have incised names, style, and glaze numbers marked on the back or bottom.

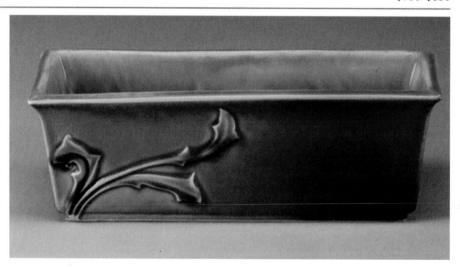

Experimental rectangular planter
in the style of Thorn Apple, unmarked, 4″ by 10″.
$225-$275

Carved experimental urn
on a high-glaze Tuscany blank, with impressed floral pattern in orange and green on a butter yellow ground, marked with glaze codes on bottom, 8 1/4″ by 7″.

$1,800

Experimental urn
decorated with band of blossoms, covered in a deep amber glaze with dark green interior, stilt-pull to base, numbered marks, 7″ by 7 1/2″.

$3,250

Experimental gourd-shaped vase
with two angular handles, decorated with laurel leaves in blue-green over a mottled raspberry glaze, marked with glaze codes on bottom, 5 1/2″ by 5 1/4″.

$2,100

Experimental vase
with painted Baneda-type design on a mottled brown and orange ground, possibly hand-thrown, touched-up fleck to one handle, unmarked, 4 1/2″ by 7″.

$1,000-$1,200

Lady Slipper hand-carved experimental vase
with yellow and white flowers on one side and a single flower with reverse coloration on the back, pink shading to sky blue, three sets of trial numbers for glaze, 8″ tall.

$4,000

Experimental vase
in Mountain Laurel pattern, with white blossoms, green leaves and pink buds on a striated band of dull green set on a tan background, with glaze number written on bottom, 9 1/8″ tall.

$3,000-$3,500

Experimental vase
with lavender geranium and leaves on a textured green and tan background, inscribed on reverse "Geranium" and marked on bottom with glaze numbers, 9 1/4″ by 8 1/4″.

$2,500-$2,800

Lady Slipper experimental vase
with yellow and lavender flowers on a textured and smooth background of dusty green and tan, with glaze numbers on bottom and gold foil label, 8 1/4″ tall.

$2,800-$3,200

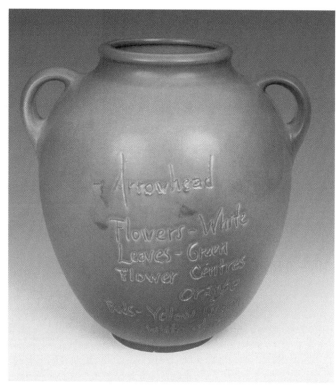

Experimental vase

in the Arrowhead pattern, white blossoms and green leaves on a textured and smooth background of dusty blue, inscribed on reverse, "Arrowhead ... Flowers-white ... Leaves-green ... Flower centres orange ... Buds yellow green white edges," with glaze numbers written on bottom, 8 7/8" tall.

`$3,000-$3,500

Trial glaze two-handled bulbous vase

covered in a shaded blue, green, and ochre matte glaze, shallow 1 1/2" scratch to body, unmarked, 9 1/4" by 8 1/4".

$500-$600

Trial glaze plate

with series of numbers representing color codes, 8" diameter.

$1,800

Falline

Still one of the most popular designs, Falline (early 1930s) is ringed by heavy sinuous forms separated in the middle by a pea-pod pattern that can be green, bluish, or yellow. Body colors include various shades of mottled pinkish-tan darkening to brown, and yellow-green blending with blue. Pieces are unmarked or have foil labels.

Falline blue bulbous vase
with collared rim and curved handles, glaze inconsistency to one side, good mold and color, unmarked, 6 1/4″ by 6 1/4″.

$850-$950

Falline blue low bowl
touch-up to handle and to rim, unmarked, 9 1/4″ diameter.

$150-$200

Falline blue ovoid two-handled vase
unmarked, 7 1/4″ by 5 1/2″.

$1,000-$1,200

Falline blue bulbous two-handled vase
two minor bruises and a small repaired chip, all to one handle, unmarked, 7 1/2″ tall.

$750-$850

Falline blue two-handled vase
Y-shaped crack through body, foil label, 6 3/4″ by 5″.

$325-$375

Falline brown bulbous two-handled vase
foil label, 6 1/2″ by 6 1/2″.

$550-$650

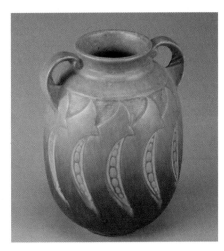

Falline brown bulbous two-handled vase
unmarked, 7 1/2″ tall.

$525-$575

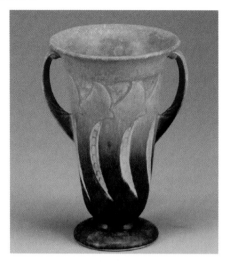

Falline brown two-handled vase
unmarked, 8 1/2″ by 6″.

$450-$550

Falline brown flaring urn
unmarked, 6 1/4″ tall.

$350-$450

Pair of Falline brown urns
crack from rim and 1/2″ chip to base of one, 1/4″ chip to base of other, remnant of store labels, 8 1/2″ by 7″.

$550-$650/pair

Falline brown bulbous vase
with crisp mold, 1/2″ chip to base, unmarked, 15 1/4″ by 7 1/4″.

$1,100-$1,300

Falline brown bulbous two-handled vase
unmarked, 6 1/2″ by 6 3/4″.

$500-$600

Falline blue bulbous two-handled vase
unmarked, 6 1/4″ by 4 3/4″ by 3 3/8″.

$950-$1,100

Falline brown bulbous two-handled vase
gold paper label and obscured ink stamp, one handle broken and badly repaired, 6 1/8″ by 5″ by 3 1/2″.

$250-$300

Falline brown two-handled vessel
with squat base, stabilized 4″ Y-shaped lines from rim, restored shallow chip at base, remnant of foil label, 12 1/2″ by 7″.

$1,200-$1,400

Falline brown bulbous handled vase
(644-6″), 6 3/8″ by 6 1/4″ by 5 3/4″.

$900-$1,000

Ferella

Named for designer Frank Ferrell, the Ferella line (1931) features pierced borders and footed bases, both decorated with tiny stylized floral motifs that at first appear to be a shell pattern. Exterior colors include mottled brown and tan with pink or lavender hues, and raspberry red combined with green. Pieces are unmarked or have paper labels.

Ferella brown oval centerpiece bowl
1˝ line from rim to cutout, unmarked, 5 1/2˝ by 13˝.
$650-$750

Pair of Ferella brown candlesticks
black paper label on one, 4 1/2˝ tall each.
$350-$450

Ferella brown center bowl
with built-in flower frog, black paper label, 9 1/2˝ diameter.
$525-$625

Ferella brown footed ovoid vase
unmarked, 10 1/4˝ by 6˝.
$850-$950

Ferella brown bud vase
unmarked, 6˝ by 4 1/2˝.
$300-$400

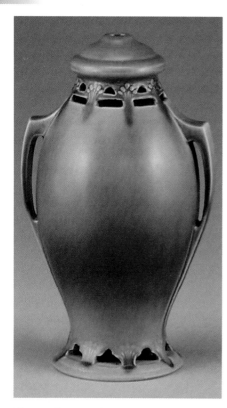

Green factory lamp base
in the style of Ferella, restoration to top, remnant of foil label, 10 1/2″ tall.

$800-$900

Ferella red flaring vase
restorations to rim and base, unmarked, 8 1/2″ by 4 3/4″.

$300-$350

Ferella brown vessel
with flaring rim, remnant of black paper label, 5″ by 6 3/4″.

$550-$650

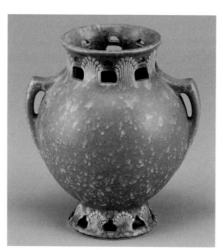

Ferella red bulbous urn
short tight line to rim, black paper label, 8″ by 7 1/2″.

$750-$850

Ferella red flaring vase
unmarked, 5 1/4″ by 4 1/4″.

$500-$600

Two Ferella red pieces
footed oval bowl with restoration to two long lines from rim, and squat vessel, unmarked; 5 1/2″ by 12 3/4″, and 4″ by 6 1/2″.

$650-$750/pair

Ferella red bud vase
unmarked, 6″ by 4 1/2″.

$600-$700

Ferella red beehive-shaped vessel
unmarked, 5 3/4″ by 6 3/4″.

$800-$900

Florane I and II

There is some lingering debate as to the correct term for these two patterns. Some prefer to include Florane I with Rosecraft; others call Florane II "Etruscan." Three decades and a world of style difference separate the two. Florane I (circa 1920) did borrow from the classical Rosecraft shapes, but has more colors. Florane II (1949) has several billowing, twisted profiles and brighter hues. The former has ink stamps, the latter has raised marks.

Florane I flaring ovoid vase
"Rv" ink stamp, in a style also found in Lustre and Rosecraft-Color, 9″ by 8″.

$110-$140

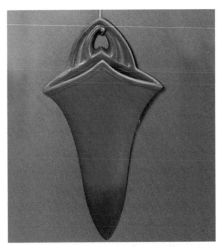

Florane I brown wall pocket
touch-up to tip, "Rv" ink stamp, in a style also found in Rosecraft-Color, 9 1/2″.

$90-$110

Two Florane I baskets
both with "Rv" ink stamp, right: Rosecraft shape 310/9, 9 7/8″ tall; left: Rosecraft shape 319/8, 8 3/8″.

$350-$450 each

Two Florane I pieces
vase (Rosecraft shape 244/6), "Rv" ink stamp, 6″ tall, $200 to $250; low bowl (124/6) with separate flower frog (15/3 1/2); bowl 2 1/8″ tall, 7 1/4″ diameter, bowl marked with "Rv" stamp, frog unmarked.

$250-$300/pair

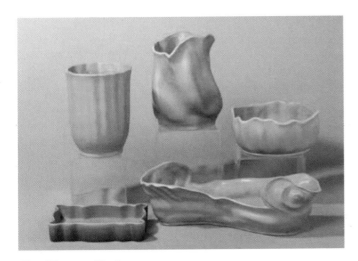

Five Florane II pieces
blue planter (64-12″), two green vases (81-7″ and 80-6″), green planter (60-6″), and tan rectangular dish (407-6″), all marked.

$225-$275/set

Five Florane II planters
(94-8″, 90-4″, 72-5″ and 73-6″), four in matte blue and one in glossy beige, all marked.

$100-$125/set

Florentine

Florentine had two incarnations, first in 1924 and again in 1940, sometimes called Florentine I and II. The earlier version comes in brown and ivory, and has rough textured brown panels regularly spaced and separated by garlands of grape vines and flowers, with a modified egg-and-dart rim. Pieces are unmarked or have an "Rv" ink stamp. The later version has textured brown and ivory panels separated by ivory partitions with green-glazed decoration and a green-trimmed rim. These pieces are unmarked or have a raised "Roseville U.S.A." mark.

Florentine brown hanging basket
"Rv" ink stamp, 4″ by 7″.

$125-$150

Florentine brown jardinière
with chip to one handle, unmarked, 8″ by 11″.

$250-$350

Florentine brown "gate" double candleholder
unmarked, 9″ by 4 1/2″ by 2 3/4″.

$120-$140

Two Florentine brown jardinières
several chips and lines to both, repair to one; "Rv" ink stamp to one, 9″ by 12 1/2″ and 8 1/2″ by 11″.

$200-$250/pair

Two Florentine pieces
ivory footed dish (some minor bruises and nicks to rim, a few small chips to body) and brown jardinière (bruise to one flower, chip and line to base), one marked, 4″ by 10″ and 7″ by 9 1/2″.

$90-$110/pair

Florentine brown jardinière
several small nicks, chips, and lines, unmarked, 10 1/4″ by 14″.

$125-$175

Florentine brown jardinière and pedestal

several minor hairlines, touch-ups to decoration, and restoration to both handles on jardinière; glaze inconsistencies around base of pedestal; jardinière:10 1/2″ tall; pedestal: 18 1/2″ tall.

$900-$1,200

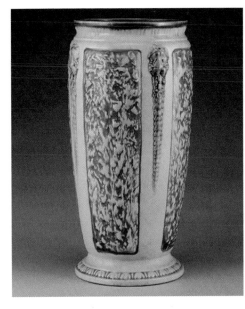

Florentine ivory umbrella stand

minor glaze burst near base and short tight spider line to underside of base (does not go through), unmarked, 20 1/2″ by 10″.

$275-$325

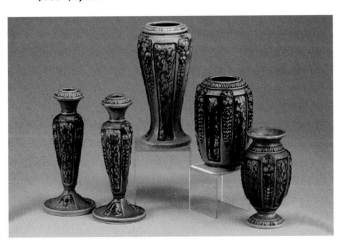

Five Florentine brown pieces

bulbous vase (a couple minute flecks), corseted vase (small chip and a line), another bulbous vase, and two candlesticks (reglued base and bruise to rim of one), "Rv″ ink stamp to four; tallest: 8 1/2″.

$250-$300/set

Four Florentine brown pieces

bulbous vase, conical vessel, and two double bud vases; several lines, chips, and nicks to each, "Rv″ ink stamp to three; tallest: 12″.

$150-$200/set

Four Florentine pieces

brown vase with minor nick, brown compote with several cracks from rim, ivory hanging basket with some nicks, and a brown jardinière in as-is condition (repairs, chips, etc.), some marked; jardinière: 6 1/2″ tall.

$150-$200/set

Four Florentine brown vases

8 1/2″ vase in as-is condition; several small chips and bruises to the others, all marked; heights: 10 1/2″, 8 1/2″, 7 1/2″, and 6 1/2″.

$225-$275/set

Foxglove

One of the most naturalistic patterns, Foxglove (1942) features tall, tapering blossom clusters of dusty white, pink, and yellow with green leaves on backgrounds of blue, green, and pink-brown. Pieces usually feature raised marks that say "Roseville U.S.A."

Foxglove blue hanging basket
with two pointed handles, stamped "U.S.A.," 5 1/2"
by 10".

$175-$200

Foxglove blue wall pocket
(1292-8") with strong mold and color, minor nick
to one flower, raised mark.

$350-$375

Pair of Foxglove blue bookends
bruise to bottom corner of one, raised U.S.A. mark, 6" by 5 1/2".
$125-$175

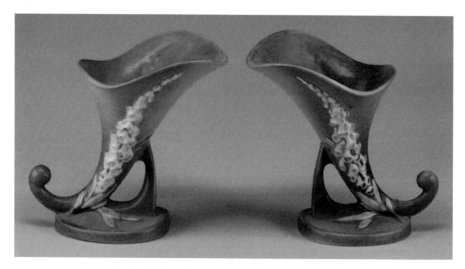

Pair of Foxglove green cornucopia vases
(164-8"), reglued tip to one, raised marks.

$125-$175

Foxglove green vase
(55-16"), several flat chips to flowers and base
(some possibly in making), raised mark.

$325-$375

Two Foxglove pieces
a blue shell-shaped planter (426-6″) with nicks to one end, and a
green urn (162-8″) with line to one flower, both marked.

$250-$300/pair

Foxglove blue bulbous vase
(418-4″) with chip to each handle and crack to one, raised mark.

$60-$70

Four Foxglove green pieces
43-6″, 44-6″ (repair under rim), 161-6″ (bruise to handle), and 42-4″, all
marked.

$275-$325/set

Two Foxglove green pieces
shell-shaped vessel with line and chips to rim, and vase (48-8″), raised marks.

$110-$140

Foxglove pink basket
(373-8"), minute nick to one flower, raised mark.
$150-$200

Foxglove pink jardinière
(418-6"), raised mark, 6 1/2" by 8 3/4" by 8 1/4".
$225-$250

Two Foxglove pink pieces
console bowl (425-14") with chip and fleck to tip and a
cornucopia vase (163-6") with minor peppering, raised marks.
$200-$250/pair

Two Foxglove pink vases
166-6" and 161-6", raised marks.
$200-$250/pair

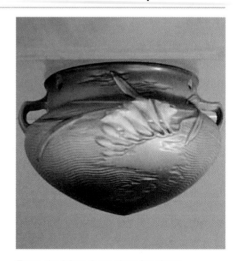

Freesia blue hanging basket
minor glaze scaling to a few high points, stamped
USA, 5 1/2" by 7 3/4".
$150-$175

Freesia

Introduced in 1945, Freesia features
rather stylized blossoms in fanning
clusters of white, lavender, and yellow
wrapped around the body of the
vessels. Backgrounds are blended blues,
brown-orange-russet, and greens. Most
are marked—often raised, sometimes
impressed.

Foxglove pink wall pocket
(1292-8"), raised mark.
$225-$275

Freesia blue basket
(390-7˝), 8 1/4˝ by 7 3/8˝ by 3 5/8˝.

$300-$350

Two Freesia pieces
blue basket (392-10˝) with restored chip at base,
and brown flowerpot (670-5˝), raised marks.
$125-$175/pair

Three Freesia blue pieces
tall ewer (21-15˝) with minor bruise near spout, flaring vase (124-9˝)
with 1/4˝ chip to rim, and smaller vase (119-7˝), all marked.
$400-$450/set

Four Freesia pieces
pair of brown candlesticks (61-4 1/2˝), blue planter (463-5˝) with line and
restored chips at rim, and large blue bowl (469-14˝) with some minor firing
bursts at rim and line through underside of base (does not go through), raised
marks.
$125-$175/set

Freesia blue cookie jar
(4-8″), 1/2 inch bruise to rim and lid, a few small
glaze nicks to high points (some from firing),
raised mark.

$400-$450

Freesia blue creamer
(6C) and sugar (6S), raised marks; creamer, 4 1/2″ by 4 1/4″ by 2 7/8″; sugar, 5 1/8″ by 4 3/4″ by 2 1/2″.

$150-$170/pair

Freesia blue tea set
(6), raised marks; teapot: 7 1/2″ by 11″.

$350-$400/set

Two Freesia pieces
blue flaring vase (125-10″) with restored chips to
rim and green console bowl (466-10″) with light
scaling to rim, raised marks.

$90-$110/pair

Four Freesia pieces
two brown ewers (20-10″) with nick to one, blue
vase (125-10″) with chips, and brown vase
(122-8″), all marked.

$275-$325/set

**Freesia brown lamp base and
fittings**
bruise to one handle, no visible mark; pottery: 13″
tall.

$400-$450

Three Freesia pieces
brown urn (196-8″), blue ewer (19-6″), and blue
bud vase (196-7″), all marked.

$275-$325/set

Five Freesia brown pieces
basket (392-10″), wall pocket (1296-8″) with
hairline and chips, pitcher (19-6″), and pair of low
candlesticks (1160-2″), all marked.

$325-$375/set

Freesia brown bulbous vase
(128-15″), restoration to rim, raised mark.

$350-$400

if perfect, otherwise

$175-$225

Freesia brown bulbous vase
(463-5″), raised mark, 5 1/8″ by 8 1/4″ by 7″.

$100-$125

Freesia brown flaring two-handled vase
(124-9″), base chip, 9 1/2″ by 7 3/8″ by 4 5/8″.

$300-$350

Three Freesia pieces
brown pitcher (20-10″), green vase (123-9″) with repair to rim and flat chip at base, and green squat pitcher (19-6″), raised marks.

$250-$300/set

Freesia brown flaring two-handled vase
(122-8″), raised mark, 8 1/4″ by 5 5/8″.

$225-$250

Freesia brown two-handled vase
(125-10″), raised mark, 10 1/4″ by 5 3/4″.

$175-$225

Two Freesia green pieces
urn (127-12″) and two-handled vase (121-8″), raised marks.

$350-$400/pair

Freesia brown two-handled vase
with bulbous base (126-10″), raised mark, 10 1/4″
by 6 1/4″.

$125-$150

Three Freesia green pieces
low bowl (465-8″) with poorly repaired chip to handle, vase (119-7″), and squat ewer (19-6″), all marked.

$175-$225/set

Freesia green tall ewer
(21-15″), firing line to rim, two 1/2″ chips to base,
raised mark.

$250-$300

Three Freesia green pieces
pitcher (20-10″) with flat chip to base, small bowl (464-6″), and center bowl (467-10″) with 1/4″ chip and
fleck to rim, all marked.

$225-$275/set

Freesia green jardinière
(669-8″) with some glaze nicks to rim, raised mark.
$200-$250

Two Freesia green pieces
console bowl (468-12″) and urn (123-9″); fleck to rim of bowl, tight line and 1/4″ bruise to rim of urn, both marked.

$150-$200/pair

Freesia green cookie jar
(4-8″), several small chips on bottom ring, raised mark.
$275-$300

Freesia green two-handled vase
(117-6″), raised mark, base chip, 6 1/4″ by 5 1/8″ by 3 5/8″.
$90-$110

Freesia green wall pocket
(1296-3″), raised mark, 8 1/8″ by 6 1/2″ by 3″.
$275-$325

Three Freesia pieces
green planter (669-4″) with chip to one handle, green pillow vase (199-6″), and blue cornucopia-shaped vase (198-8″), all marked.
$200-$250/set

Four Freesia pieces
green bud vase (195-7″) with two small glaze misses to neck, green pillow vase (199-6″), and a pair of brown book-shaped bookends (15) with restoration to edges on both, raised marks.
$250-$300/set

Fuchsia

A strikingly simple design, Fuchsia (1938) features small hanging flowers and large heart-shaped leaves on backgrounds that are both smooth and textured. Most collectors refer to the colors simply as blue, brown, and green, but the body colors vary from amber-pink-brown to blue-white, to a mix of olive and forest green shot with dark salmon tones. Pieces usually have impressed marks.

Fuchsia blue hanging basket
with three handles, unmarked, 5 1/2″ by 6 1/2″.
$350-$375

Three-piece Fuchsia blue console set
consisting of a bowl (349-8″) with painted-over nick inside rim and a pair of candlesticks (113-2″), all marked.
$250-$300/set

Fuchsia blue bowl
(348-5″), impressed mark.
$125-$175

Fuchsia blue console set
(351-10″ and 113-2″) with strong mold and color, 1″ bruise to bowl, impressed marks.
$375-$400/set

Fuchsia blue center bowl
(353-14″), impressed mark.
$225-$275

Fuchsia blue flowerpot with under plate
(646-5″), under plate may not match, minor glaze scale to one flower, impressed mark.
$300-$325

Fuchsia blue console set
consisting of a bowl (353-14˝) with minute fleck to base and 1/4˝ chip to one leaf, and a pair of candlesticks (113-5˝), all marked.

$275-$325/set

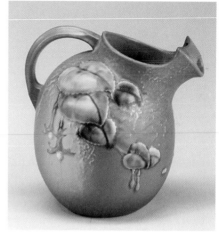

Fuchsia blue water pitcher with ice lip
(1322), impressed mark, 8˝.

$400-$500

Three Fuchsia blue pieces
pair of small jardinières (645-3˝) and cornucopia vase (129-6˝), impressed marks.

$300-$350/set

Fuchsia blue bulbous planter
(645-4˝), impressed mark.

$150-$200

Fuchsia blue bulbous jardinière
(645-6˝) with strong mold and brilliant color, impressed mark.

$300-$350

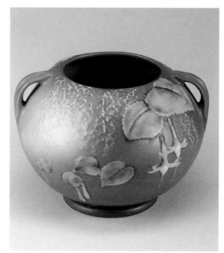

Fuschia blue spherical planter
(347-6˝), impressed mark.

$275-$325

Fuchsia blue bulbous vase with ribbed neck
(891-6˝), line and minute fleck to one handle, impressed mark.

$150-$200

Three Fuchsia brown pieces
pair of candlesticks (1132) with nick to one, flat chip to base of the other, and bulbous planter with faint spider lines to base and glaze misses; planter: 6˝ tall.

$175-$225/set

Fuchsia blue floor vase
(905-18˝) with crisp mold, impressed mark.
$900-$1,000

Fuchsia brown basket
(350-8˝) with attached flower frog, impressed mark.
$275-$325

Fuchsia blue vase
(903-12˝) with strong mold and color, impressed mark.
$450-$550

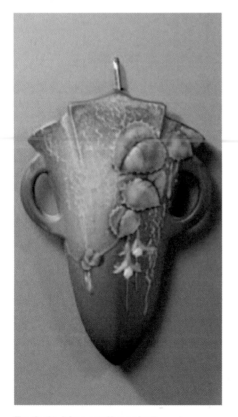

Fuchsia blue wall pocket
(1282-8˝), raised mark.
$600-$700

Fuchsia brown console set
(1133-5˝ and 350-8˝), impressed marks.
$325-$375/set

Fuchsia blue vase
with strong mold, unmarked, 9 1/4˝ tall.
$375-$425

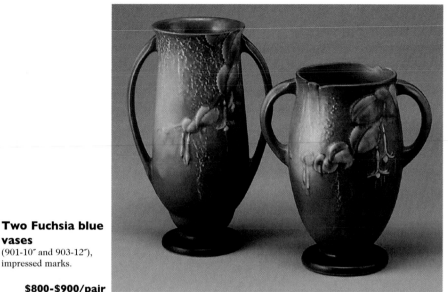

Two Fuchsia blue vases
(901-10″ and 903-12″), impressed marks.

$800-$900/pair

Fuchsia brown jardinière
with crisp mold and good color, unmarked, 6 3/4″ by 9 1/2″.

$150-$200

Fuchsia brown bulbous planter
obscured impressed mark, 5 1/2″ by 8″.

$175-$225

Fuchsia handled vase
(346-4″), 4″ by 6 1/2″.

$300-$350

Fuchsia green center bowl
(350-8″), hairline through base and minute fleck to one handle, impressed mark.

$90-$110

Fuchsia brown pitcher
(1322), peppering to body, impressed mark, 8″ by
8 1/2″.

$350-$400

Fuchsia brown bulbous vase
minute pock mark and shallow spider line to base
does not go through, obscured impressed mark,
8 1/4″ by 6″.

$110-$140

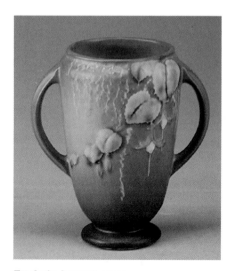

Fuchsia brown vase
(873-6″), impressed mark.

$125-$175

Fuchsia brown floor vase
(905-18″) with good mold and color, raised mark.

$850-$950

Fuchsia green two-handled vase
(900-9″), impressed mark, 9 3/8″ by 6 1/4″ by 4
3/8″.

$225-$250

Fuchsia green vase
(illegible mark) with 1/2″ tight line to rim,
impressed mark.

$275-$300

Fuchsia green vase
(904-15″) with good mold and color, impressed
mark.

$650-$750

Pair of Fuchsia bulbous two-handled vases
(691-6″), one brown and one green, silver foil label.
$300-$350/pair

Fuchsia green pitcher
(1322), several flecks overall and restoration to rim, impressed mark, 9″ by 8 1/2″.
$200-$250

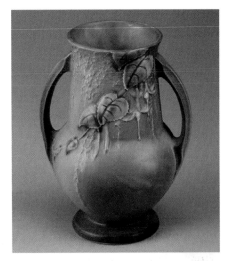

Fuchsia green bulbous vase
(898-8″), minor abrasion at rim, raised mark.
$150-$200

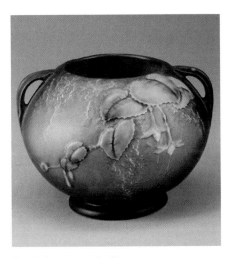

Fuchsia green bulbous vase
(34-7″), minor peppering near rim, impressed mark.
$150-$200

Fuchsia green bulbous vase
faint impressed mark, 8 1/2″ by 6 1/2″.
$110-$140

Fuchsia green two-handled vase
faint impressed mark, 7 1/2″ by 6″.
$125-$175

Fuchsia green flaring two-handled vessel
obscured impressed mark, 6 1/2″ by 5 1/2″.
$110-$140

Two green Fuchsia vessels
squat vessel (346-4″) with minute fleck to rim and a small bulbous planter, one marked; taller: 4 1/2″.
$250-$300/pair

Three Fuchsia pieces
pair of brown candlesticks (1132) with flecks to one, and green vase (894-7″), all marked.
$175-$225/set

Fudji

Unlike Fujiyama and Woodland, which were also the creations of Gazo Foudji, this pattern from the first decade of the 20th century has symmetrical, stylized art nouveau patterns—with suggestions of Persian influence—on similarly shaped vessels, and Rozane Ware wafers.

Fujiyama/ Woodland

Designed by Gazo Foudji, the wares are closely related. Introduced in 1905-06, these pieces have delicate glazed floral motifs on a textured, buff-colored body. The Fujiyama pieces have an ink stamp, while Woodland pieces have a Rozane/ Woodland wafer. Fujiyama should not be confused with Fudji, which has symmetrical, stylized art nouveau patterns on similarly shaped vessels, plus Rozane Ware wafers.

Fujiyama bud vase
decorated with a poppy, 1/2" chip and glaze flakes to base, marked Fujiyama, 5 1/4" tall.
$375-$425

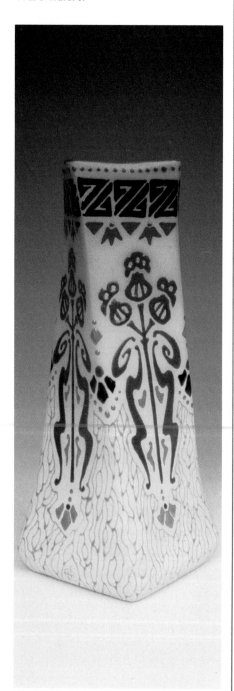

Fudji four-sided and twisted vase
(shape R 5), Rozane Ware wafer, 9 3/4" tall.
$2,800-$3,200

Fujiyama classically shaped vase
decorated with white blossoms, glaze flaking to top and bottom, hairline to rim, Fujiyama ink stamp, 8 1/2" by 4 1/4".
$325-$375

Fujiyama cylindrical vase
with brown daylilies, restoration to some small areas of enamel, Fujiyama ink stamp, 15" by 4".
$1,800-$2,000

Fujiyama vase
decorated with freesia and falling leaves, some minute flecks to decoration, chips around base, Fujiyama ink stamp, 10" by 3".
$500-$600

Woodland bud vase
with poppies, restoration to rim and base, touch-up to decoration, unmarked, 6" by 1 3/4".
$175-$225

Woodland bud vase
short (firing?) line to rim, round Rozane seal, 6 1/2" by 2 1/4".
$275-$325

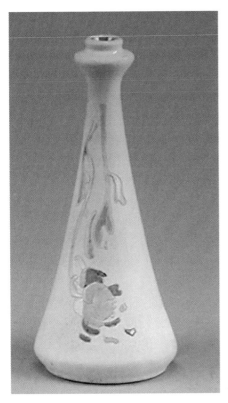

Woodland bottle-shaped vase
incised with stylized flower in yellow and amber on a bisque ground, Rozane wafer, 8˝ by 3 1/2˝.

$450-$550

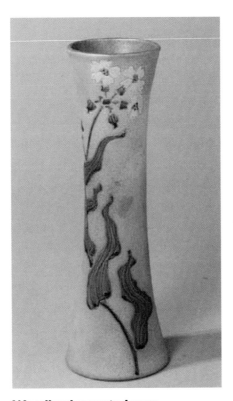

Woodland corseted vase
enamel-decorated with white blossoms and green leaves, restoration to chip at rim, Rozane Ware/ Woodland wafer, 10˝ by 3˝.

$475-$525

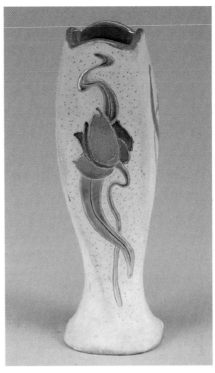

Woodland four-sided vase
decorated with brown flowers and stylized leaves, fleck and very short, tight line to rim, minor flat chips at base, marked "ROZANE WARE," 8 3/4˝ by 2 1/2˝.

$250-$300

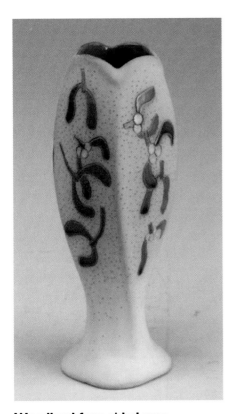

Woodland four-sided vase
decorated with mistletoe, Rozane Woodland wafer, 8 3/4˝.

$800-$900

Woodland bulbous vase
decorated with glossy brown poppies and leaves on an ivory bisque base, 1/2˝ chip at base, line inside rim does not go through, and slight firing burst to one petal, marked "Rozane Ware Woodland," incised "ED," and "ET" written along base, 16 1/4˝ by 6˝.

$1,100-$1,300

Woodland vase
with naturalistic floral motif, shape W-974, Rozane Ware Woodland wafer, 10 1/2˝ tall.

$750-$850

Futura

Futura is a striking blend of art deco and floral designs, both naturalistic and stylized. Introduced in 1924, everything was fair game, and previously unknown colors, shapes, and glaze combinations continue to emerge. Pieces are unmarked or have a black paper label.

Futura hanging basket
with pastel leaves on an orange ground, glaze flake to one edge, repair to another flake, unmarked, 5″ by 7 1/2″.
$150-$200

Futura six-sided center bowl
with geometric designs in brown and orange glaze, touch-up to minor chip on one rim corner, unmarked, 4″ by 8″.

$250-$300

Futura faceted center bowl
with blossoms, the interior covered in an orange glaze, the exterior in mottled blue, minor glaze miss to rim, unmarked, 3 3/4″ by 12″.

$500-$600

Futura polygonal bowl
with restoration to rim, unmarked, 4″ by 8″.
$225-$275

Pair of Futura candlesticks
with orange, green, and blue geometric pattern, one has small chip to base, black label, 4″ by 3 1/4″.

$650-$750

Futura chalice
in two shades of glossy green, restoration to stilt-pull chip, 2″ hairline from rim, black paper label, very rare, 5 3/4″ by 3 1/2″.

$1,400-$1,600

Futura jardinière
with pink and purple stylized leaves on a green ground, several small glaze misses to decoration, unmarked, 6″ by 8 1/2″.

$200-$250

Futura jardinière and pedestal
with leaves in pastel tones on a brown ground, jardinière with cracks and holes (as is), the pedestal with small bruises and glaze flakes, possibly from firing, unmarked; jardinière: 10″ tall; pedestal: 18″ tall.

$250-$300

Futura console set
with floral motif, including faceted flaring bowl, flower frog, and pair of candlesticks; pair of shallow exterior lines to one candlestick that do not go through, black paper label on one candlestick; bowl: 3 1/2″ by 12 1/4″, candlesticks: 4 1/4″ tall.

$650-$750/set

Futura jardinière and pedestal
with pastel leaves on an orange ground, small burst to shoulder and spider lines to base of jardinière; restoration around rim, touch-ups, 3 1/2″ line to base, and flat chip to bottom of pedestal, unmarked; jardinière: 10″ by 15″; pedestal: 18 1/2″ by 11 1/4″.

$400-$500

Futura jardinière
with pastel leaves on an orange ground, bruises to handles, hairlines and reglued chips to bottom, small chip to shoulder, unmarked, 9″ by 13 1/2″.

$150-$200

Futura jardinière
decorated with spade-shaped leaves, unmarked, 7″ by 10 1/2″.

$400-$450

Two Futura pink pieces

buttressed pillow planter with blossoms (touch-up to glaze flake) and a flaring four-sided vase with green "V" pattern (chips to two corners and around base), both unmarked, 4 1/2″ tall and 7″ tall.

$275-$325/pair

Futura faceted pedestal vase

(412-9″, known as "The Tank"), in streaked tan over blue, unmarked, 9 1/2″ by 8 3/4″.

$14,000-$15,000

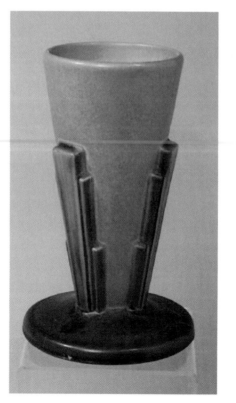

Futura pink urn

with restoration to base, unmarked, 8 1/4″ by 5 3/4″.

$450-$500

Futura conical vase

with three buttresses in orange and green, unmarked, 8″ by 5″.

$650-$750

Futura vase

(392-10″) with round stepped base and square flaring neck, in green and dusty blue-gray, unmarked.

$800-$900

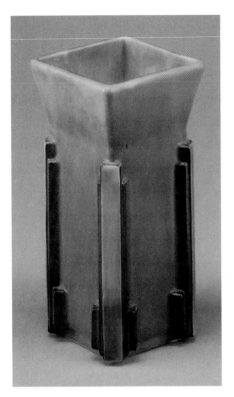

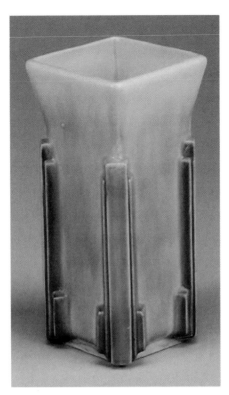

Futura four-sided vase
(#402) in orange and blue with green buttresses to
each corner, some tiny nicks to edges, unmarked,
8 1/4″ by 3 3/4″.

$600-$700

Futura four-sided vase
(#402) with green buttresses on a pale blue to
beige ground, 1/2″ tight line to rim and 1/4″ chip to
bottom of one buttress, unmarked, 8″ by 3 3/4″.

$500-$600

Futura four-sided vase
with buttressed handles, stacked neck, and
triangles, all covered in pink and green glossy
glazes, chips to three corners at base, unmarked,
8 1/4″ by 6″.

$350-$400

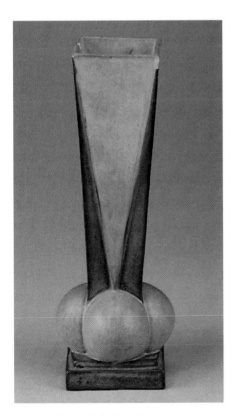

Futura four-sided vase
with lobed base, chips to rim, bruise and writing to
base, 12″ tall.

$450-$550

Futura two-handled vase
with bulbous base and stacked neck, covered in
a bright green and charcoal semi-matte glaze,
unmarked, 9″ by 5″.

$800-$900

Futura pink twisted vase
with blue and green geometric designs at rim,
unmarked, 8 1/4″ by 3 1/2″.

$550-$650

Futura blue pillow vase
in the "Sunray" pattern, unmarked, repaired chip, 6″ by 2 3/4″ by 5 1/4″.

$250-$300

Futura pink pillow vase
with small branches, minute glaze fleck at rim, unmarked, 4″ by 6 1/4″.

$200-$250

Futura bulbous vase
with stepped neck, covered in green glaze with darker green geometric design, drilled for lamp base, abrasion around rim, remnant of paper label, 10″ by 7 3/4″.

$275-$325

Futura bulbous vase
with stepped neck, base entirely repaired and several scratches to body, unmarked, 10″ by 7 1/2″.

$250-$300

Futura bottle-shaped vase
with stepped neck in green and brown, several chips to base, remnant of black paper label, 9″ by 8″.

$475-$525

Futura bulbous vase
decorated with Pine Cone pattern, 1/2″ firing chip at base, unmarked, 10″ by 6″.

$800-$900

Futura twisted four-sided vase
with branches and leaves on a mottled orange to green ground, small clay pimple or kiln mark to one corner and Y-shaped line, unmarked, 6 1/2″ by 3″.

$225-$275

Futura "Lotus Ball" spherical vase
with blue and green leaves, unmarked, 7 1/2″ by 6″.

$600-$700

Futura vase
with spherical base and stepped neck, covered in green and pink semi-matte glaze, few shallow scratches and minor nick to body, unmarked, 8 1/2″ by 5″.

$375-$425

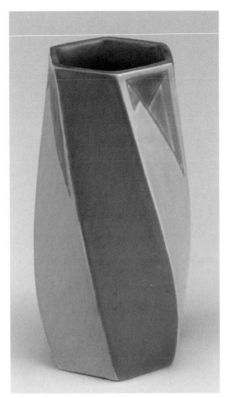

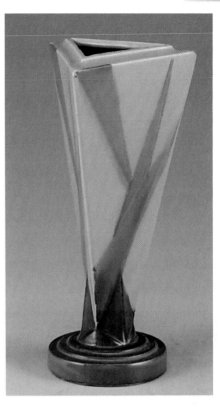

Futura star-shaped vase
(#385) in pink and green glazes, minute pinhead-sized fleck or burst to edge, unmarked, 8 1/4″ by 3 1/4″.

$300-$350

Futura six-sided twisted vase
with green and blue triangles on a two-tone matte pink base, unmarked, 8″ by 4″.

$600-$700

Futura three-sided vase
(388-9″) with blue geometric designs on a circular base, unmarked, 9 1/4″ by 4 1/2″ by 3 7/8″.

$800-$1,000

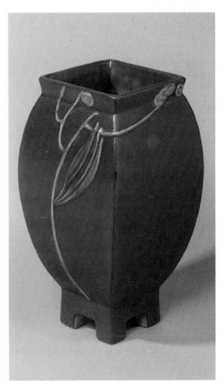

Futura two-handled vase
with green geometric band around stepped neck, minute glaze fleck to base, unmarked, 6 1/4″ by 4″.

$275-$325

Futura bottle-shaped vase
with two buttressed handles, covered in an orange and green glaze, minute fleck to one shoulder, unmarked, 7 1/4″ by 4 1/4″.

$225-$275

Futura swollen four-sided footed vessel
with stylized art deco flowers, 1/2″ glaze miss to edge, unmarked, 9 1/2″ by 5″.

$850-$950

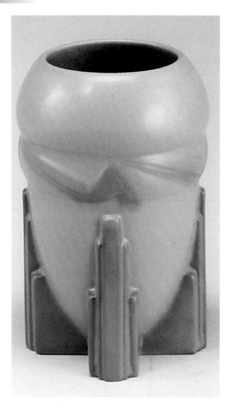

Futura blue vase
with blue-green buttressed base, some minor pock marks and chips to base, unmarked, 7 3/4˝ by 5˝.
$400-$450

Futura vase
with buttressed handles decorated with tulips on a blue, green, and yellow mottled ground, colored-in chip and repair to base, touch-ups to several small glaze chips around rim, and spider lines to base that go up side of vase, unmarked, 13˝ by 6 1/4˝.
$400-$500

Futura beehive-shaped vessel
in blue and amber glazes, two minor chips inside foot ring, unmarked, 7 1/4˝ by 5 3/4˝.
$400-$500

Futura four-sided flaring vessel
on a buttressed base, both covered in a mottled green and umber glaze, opposing lines to rim, cracks to two buttresses, chip and several flecks to base, unmarked, 4 1/4˝ by 5˝.
$250-$300

Futura two-handled vase
with orange stepped neck on a green base, small factory glazed chip to rim, unmarked, 7 1/4˝ by 4 1/2˝.
$225-$275

Two Futura pieces
small vase with squat base in orange and green and flat vase in pink with stylized flowers, black paper label to first, 7 1/2˝ by 4 1/2˝ and 4 1/4˝ by 6 1/2˝.
$500-$600/pair

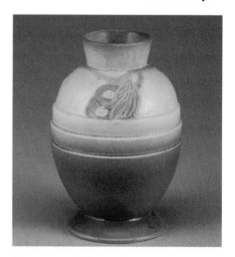

Futura ovoid vessel
with branches and blue blossoms, unmarked, 8 1/2˝ by 5 1/4˝.
$1,000-$1,200

Futura wall pocket
with stylized leaf-like design in purple, yellow, green, and blue, some small chips to tip, 8 1/2˝ tall.
$300-$350

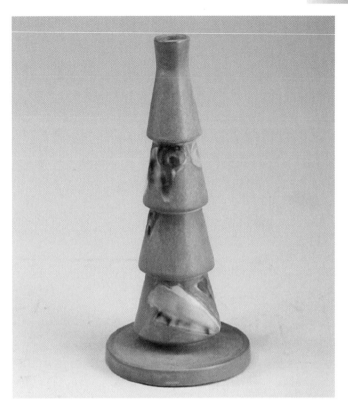

Futura tapering stacked vase
with triangles and circles in pastel tones on a burnt-orange ground, restoration to rim and minor flake to bottom, unmarked, 10 1/4″.

$375-$425

Futura spherical vessel
on trapezoidal base with polychrome circles on a green ground, 1/4″ bruise to rim, unmarked, 8 1/4″ by 6 1/2″.

$900-$1,000

Futura window box or rectangular planter
(376) in tan, dusty blue, and dark green, 15 3/4″ by 5 1/8″ by 4″.

$1,500-$1,600

Futura vase
with squat base, two handles, and a flaring faceted top in orange, brown, and blue-green, unmarked, 14 1/2″ by 5 1/4″.

$2,500-$3,500

Gardenia

Introduced in 1950, Gardenia features a wide belt of white blossoms and green leaves evenly wrapped around the vessels. Background colors are tan-brown with an orange tinge, gray, and shades of green. Pieces feature raised marks.

Gardenia brown ewer
(616-6″), raised mark, 6 1/4″ by 3″ by 3″.
$175-$225

Two Gardenia brown pieces
double bud vase (622-8″) and basket (608-8″), raised marks.
$200-$225/pair

Two Gardenia brown vases
one flaring, (687-12″) and one bulbous (688-12″) with repair to chips at base, raised marks.
$200-$250/pair

Gardenia gray hanging basket
good mold, short, tight 1″ line from rim, stamped USA, 5 1/4″ by 7 3/4″.
$90-$110

Gardenia gray basket
(609-10″), raised mark.
$200-$250

Gardenia brown ewer
(618-15″), raised mark.
$300-$350

Three Gardenia pieces
brown cornucopia-shaped vase (621-6″), green bulbous vase (685-10″), and long brown bowl (630-12″) with fleck to one edge of rim, raised marks.

$200-$250/set

Four Gardenia gray pieces
jardinière (641-5″), double vase (622-8″), and a pair of candlesticks (652-4 1/2″), all marked.

$225-$275/set

Pair of Gardenia gray double vases
(622-8″), raised marks.

$150-$200/pair

Two Gardenia vases
green bulbous (684-8″) with chip to one petal and underglaze chip at base, and brown ovoid (682-5″), both marked.

$350-$400/pair

Gardenia gray wall pocket
(666-8″), raised mark.

$300-$350

Gardenia gray vase
(689-14″), raised mark.

$250-$300

Two Gardenia pieces
gray vase (683-8″) and green spherical planter (641-5″)
glaze flake to handle of planter raised marks.

$200-$225/pair

Three Gardenia pieces
tall gray vase (687-12″), brown vase (688-8″), and small vessel (656-3″), all
marked.

$250-$300/set

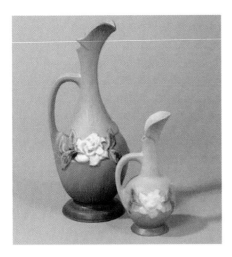

Two Gardenia pitchers
one green (617-10˝) one gray (616-6˝) raised marks.

$175-$200/pair

Pair of Gardenia green book-shaped bookends
(659), small bruise to one petal and minute spider line to edge of one, raised marks.

$110-$140/pair

Gardenia green basket
(609-10˝), raised mark.

$300-$350

Gardenia green window box
(658-8˝), raised mark, 8 3/4˝ by 3 1/8˝ by 3 1/8˝.

$125-$150

Six Gardenia green candlesticks
four low (651) and two tall (652-4 1/2˝) all marked.

$150-$200/set

German Cookware

Dating from about 1900, these wares in simple brown glazes were produced for the Romafin Pottery Co. of Chicago. Pieces also included bowls, covered casseroles, long-handled pots, and platters. All are unmarked.

German Cookware
all unmarked, teapot, 7 1/4˝ tall with lid,

coffeepot, 8 1/2˝ tall with lid; $300-$350; and creamer, 3 1/4˝ tall.

$250-$300;

$40-$50

Hexagon

From 1924, Hexagon was part of the Rosecraft line and has broad faceted shapes with an Arts & Crafts-inspired decoration. It is commonly brown and green, and rarely black or blue. It has an "Rv" ink stamp or label.

Hexagon green wall pocket
touch-up to glaze chips on back, small bruise to edge, "Rv" ink stamp, 8 1/2" tall.
$400-$450

Hexagon green double bud vase
in gate form (45-5"), "Rv" ink stamp, 5 1/4" tall.
$550-$600;

Hexagon low bowl
in green (135-5"), "Rv" ink stamp, 2 3/8" tall.
$225-$250

Hexagon vase
with lines, cracks, etc., paper label, 6 1/4" tall.
$90-$110

Hexagon vase
(8-7"), "Rv" ink stamp, 7 3/8" tall.
$350-$400;

Hexagon candlestick,
"Rv" ink stamp, 8 1/8" tall.
$150-$200

Two Hexagon vases
both with "Rv" ink stamp: 266-4″ in brown, **$100-$125;** 270-8″ in dull green, **$600-$700.**

Pair of Hexagon brown vases
1/2″ hairline to rim and some minute flecks to base of one, restoration to hairline and chip at rim of other, "Rv" ink stamp, 4 1/2″ by 6 1/2″ each.
$275-$325/pair

Hexagon green vase
1″ line from rim and flake to base, "Rv" ink stamp, 4 1/4″.
$200-$250

Home Art

Introduced before 1910, and as the name implies, Home Art was Roseville's do-it-yourself line. Pieces could be hand-painted or have transfer decoration from the factory. Most pieces are unmarked, and very few survive.

Home Art three-footed jardinière
painted with tulips on a teal and ivory ground, repaired chip inside rim, pock mark outside rim, and glaze chip to foot, unmarked, rare, 10″ by 12″.
$325-$375

Home Art flower pot
painted with flower, unmarked, 3 1/2″ tall.
$125-$150

Hyde Park

Roseville made ashtrays and cigarette boxes for the Hyde Park Company, which then resold the items for use as presentation pieces in the late 1940s and early '50s. The ashtrays have an applied copper-colored metal disk with a raised initial. Marks include "The Hyde Park," and a style number or year.

Three Hyde Park monogrammed ashtrays
one triangular and two biomorphic, several nicks overall, each marked "The Hyde Park - U.S.A."; largest: 10 1/2″ long.
$80-$90/set

Two Hyde Park monogrammed ashtrays
one yellow and one beige, both marked, 9″ diameter each.
$80-$90/pair

Imperial
I and II

There is no confusing Imperial I with Imperial II. Though both were introduced late in the first quarter of the 20th century, Imperial I has a rustic appearance, with a rough textured surface that mixes muddy green, brown, and ivory, and a stylized grape vine that has an odd pretzel-like appearance. This motif is set off by a shamrock-shaped leaf and a blue-gray blob that suggests a grape cluster, but you really have to use your imagination to see any grapes. Pieces are unmarked.

Imperial II is the later version, and many of the vessels have striking color combinations, like yellow-lavender, turquoise-pink, orange-green, or mottled amber and raspberry, often dripping or blurred together. Pieces are mostly unmarked but occasionally have paper labels.

Imperial I basket
minor fleck at edge of base, unmarked, 10 3/4˝ by 10˝.

$175-$225

Imperial I basket
unmarked, 6˝ by 7˝.

$175-$225

Imperial I basket
unmarked, 10 1/4˝ by 6˝.

$150-$200

Three Imperial I pieces
basket with 2˝ glaze scaling to rim, triple bud vase, and low bowl with hairline to rim, unmarked; 12 1/2˝ by 6˝, 7 3/4˝ by 4 1/2˝, and 2 1/2˝ by 8 1/2˝.

$250-$300/set

Imperial I hanging basket
several small chips and 1″ crack near one hole,
unmarked, 4 1/4″ by 7 3/4″.

$50-$60

Imperial I low bowl
unmarked, 7 3/4″ by 2 7/8″.

$125-$150

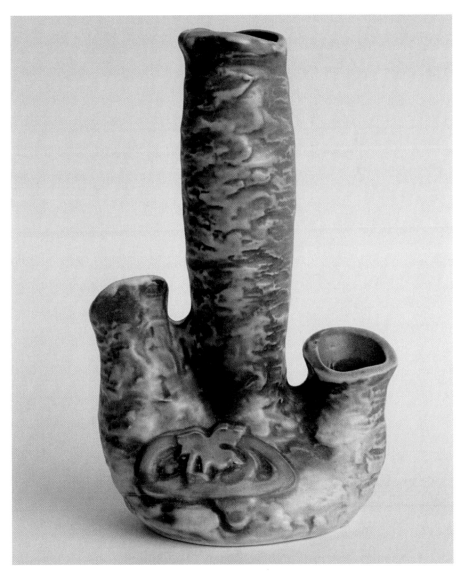

Imperial I triple vase
(29-8″), 7 5/8″ by 4 3/4″ by 3 1/2″.

$300

Imperial I bulbous vase
unmarked, 10″ by 8″.

$250-$300

Imperial I footed vessel
with closed-in rim, 1/4″ glaze pimple to body,
unmarked, 12″ by 6 1/4″.

$225-$250

Imperial II low bowl
covered in a mottled orange glaze, unmarked,
8 1/2″ diameter.

$350-$400

Imperial II beehive-shaped vase
in yellow and lavender, short tight line to rim,
unmarked, 6″ by 5 3/4″.

$200-$250

Imperial II vase
covered in a frothy turquoise glaze with yellow
band at rim, unmarked, 8″ by 7″.

$275-$325

Imperial II tapering vase
with ribbed band to body, minute fleck to body,
unmarked, 5 1/4″ by 3 1/4″.

$125-$175

Imperial II bulbous vessel
with ribbed body, covered in a purple and yellow
mottled glaze, unmarked, 6 1/4″ by 6″.

$500-$600

Imperial II vase
covered in a frothy turquoise glaze with yellow
design around rim, black paper label, 7 1/4″ by
7 1/2″.

$500-$600

Imperial II squat vessel
with embossed collar rim and green and purple mottled glaze, unmarked, 4 1/2″
by 6 1/4″.

$300-$350

**Imperial II
tapering vessel**
with ribbed body,
covered in a dripping
blue-gray over a
medium green glaze,
1/2″ kiln flaw to one
side and small stilt-pull
chip, unmarked, 5 1/4″
by 3 3/4″.

$90-$110

Imperial II wall pocket
with mottled pink and green semi-matte glaze,
black paper label, 6 1/2″ tall.
$900-$1,000

Imperial II triple wall pocket
covered in a mottled green and gold glaze, short,
tight line on edge of center holder, unmarked,
6 1/2″ tall.
$250-$350

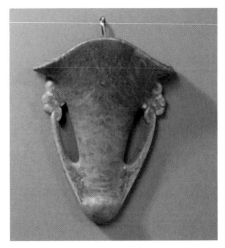

Imperial II wall pocket
covered in a mottled greenish-gold and magenta
glaze, "Rv″ ink stamp, 7 1/4″ tall.
$350-$400

Iris

Another design that faithfully mimics
nature, Iris (1939) features pairs of
large blossoms and tall, slender leaves.
Backgrounds are the familiar blue-
turquoise, salmon-brown, and dusty
pink. Pieces usually feature impressed
marks, but they are sometimes
unmarked.

Iris blue hanging basket
with two handles, some abrasion to bottom,
unmarked, 5 1/4″ by 8 1/2″.
$275-$300

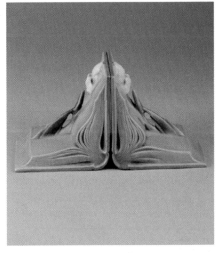

Iris blue bookends
(5), fleck to tip of one, raised marks, 5 1/4″ by 5″.
$125-$175/pair

Pair of Iris blue low candlesticks
(1134), 3/4″ glaze scale to base of one, impressed
marks, 3″ by 4″ each.
$175-$225/pair

Iris blue center or console bowl
(362-10″), impressed mark, 12 5/8″ by 6 3/4″ by 3 7/8″.
$175-$225

Iris blue flowerpot
with under plate (648-5″), 1″ bruise to rim of pot,
raised marks.

$275-$300

Iris blue footed basket planter
(355-10″), restoration to handle on one side,
impressed mark.

$150-$175

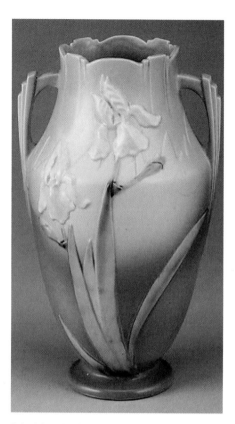

Iris blue bulbous vase
(929-15″), impressed mark.

$750-$850

Two Iris blue vases
one bud (918-7″) with small flat stilt-pull chip and
three touched-up chips, and one footed with flat
shoulder (919-7″) with minute fleck to corner of
one handle, impressed marks.

$150-$175/pair

Two Iris blue pieces
small flaring vase (914-4″) and small bowl (359-
5″) with minor pinprick to corner of one handle,
impressed marks.

$175-$200/pair

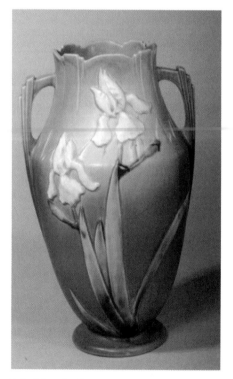

Iris blue bulbous vase
with scalloped rim (929-15″), strong mold, and
good glazing, 4″ interior body line and shallow
spider line to bottom, neither go through, and a
couple of minute flecks to rim, impressed mark.

$400-$450

Two Iris blue pieces
fan vase (922-8″) and cornucopia vase (132-8″), impressed marks.

$375-$400/pair

Iris blue flaring vase
with bulbous base, illegible impressed mark,
10 1/2" by 7 1/2".

$350-$400

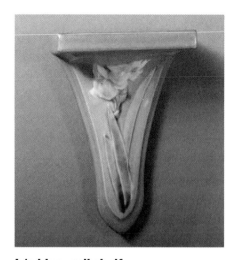

Iris blue wall shelf
(2), minute and shallow bruise to one side of shelf,
impressed mark, 8 1/4" by 5".

$450-$500

Iris brown jardinière
(647-10") and pedestal set, small reglued chip to
pedestal, nick to rim, and small filled-in chips to
flowers on jardinière, both marked.

$900-$1,000

Iris brown flaring footed urn
with squat base (823-8"), minor bruise to one
corner of handle, impressed mark.

$175-$200

Two Iris brown pieces
cornucopia vase (134-6") and small footed vessel
with squat base (130-4"), very faint impressed
mark to one.

$175-$200/pair

Iris brown wall shelf
(2), some minor bruises to petals, impressed mark,
8 1/4" by 5".

$375-$400

Two Iris brown pieces
footed pillow vase (922-8") with 1 1/2" chip to base and oval basket planter (355-10"), impressed marks.

$400-$450/pair

Iris pink console set
with oval center bowl (360-10″) and a pair of
candlesticks (1135-4 1/2″), impressed marks.
$300-$350/set

Iris pink spherical basket planter
(354-8″), impressed mark.
$250-$300

Iris brown bulbous vase
with flaring rim (920-7″), impressed mark.
$110-$140

Two Iris pieces
pink bulbous vase with flaring rim (920-7″) and
small blue urn, both marked (one illegible); urn:
4 1/4″ by 4″.
$150-$200/pair

Two Iris pink pieces
ewer (926-10″) and squat planter (647-4″) with
minor bruise to one petal, impressed marks.
$350-$400/pair

Iris pink bulbous urn
(928-12″), impressed mark.
$400-$450

Iris pink ovoid footed vase
(924-9″), strong mold and good glazing, impressed
mark.
$275-$300

Two Iris pink pieces
ovoid vase (915-5″) and small footed vessel with
squat base (130-4″), impressed marks.
$175-$200/pair

Iris pink squat vessel
unmarked, 5 1/8″ by 3 1/2″.
$160-$180

Ivory

Sometimes called Ivory II to distinguish it from the Old Ivory and Ivory Tint of 1910-12, this line from 1932 featured unadorned white vessels made in the molds of other patterns, including Donatello, Carnelian I, Foxglove, and Luffa, to name just a few. The markings vary, and some pieces have labels.

Seven Ivory II pieces
low bowl (152-6″) with bruise to base; flaring vase (260-8″) on Russco blank (repairs); larger flaring bowl on Russco blank (cracks); small planter; tall vase on Savona blank (flecks to base); bowl (266-6″) on Velmoss blank (cracks and chips); and cornucopia vase (106-7″) with flat chip to base.
$110-$140/set

Seven Ivory II candlesticks
two on faceted bases, three spherical, and two tall, one of which has an unusual blue-glazed rim, some marked.
$150-$200/set

Ivory II ewer vase in a Carnelian I shape
(1315-15″), 15″ by 8 1/8″ by 5 3/4″.
$400-$500

Five Ivory II pieces
squat planter (several hairlines, probably in firing); flaring 9″ vase; small vase; large bulbous vase (chip to handle); and smaller bulbous vase, some impressed marks, large bulbous vase: 8 1/2″ tall.
$150-$200/set

Nine Ivory II pieces
including several vases and a basket, some chips, but overall excellent condition, some marked.
$400-$450/set

Roseville Pottery Warman's
127

Ivory (Old)

Dating from the first decade of the 20th century, the Old Ivory line features geometric patterns, and floral motifs both stylized and naturalistic, on creamy-colored vessels—most often jardinières—with dark backgrounds of brown or tan. Unmarked, or with paper labels

Old Ivory jardinière
with leafy and floral motif (503), impressed mark, 7 3/4″ tall.
$350-$450

Ivory (Tinted)

An atypical design for the Roseville creamwares, Tinted Ivory features Greek Key patterns and scrolls on a group of teapots, creamers, and sugar bowls, plus floral bands on tall tankards and mugs, and even smoker sets. Bisque vessels are accented with colors that include pale yellow, blue, green, and pink. All are unmarked.

Tinted Ivory double bud vase
in gate form, unmarked, 5″ tall by 6 3/4″ wide,
$200-$250;
and a teapot, unmarked, 4 3/8″ tall.
$100-$125

Tinted Ivory footed planter and liner;
unmarked planter is 4″ tall, liner (shape 515) is 3″ tall.
$250-$300/pair

Ixia

Victorian gardeners associated the Ixia with happiness, and this line from 1937 reflects the company's robust business as the country emerged from the Depression (Roseville sales and production peaked just a few years later). The stylized blossoms seem to be blowing in the wind on backgrounds of green, pink-green, and yellow-brown. Marks are impressed.

Two Ixia green pieces with buttressed handles
hemispheric bowl (325-5″) with 1/4″ chip to one handle and ovoid vase (855-7″) with crisp mold (minute fleck to rim), impressed marks.
$125-$150/pair

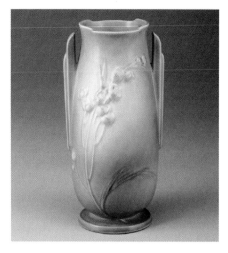

Ixia green vase
(064-12″), some peppering to body, impressed mark, and remnant of foil label to body.
$110-$140

Two Ixia pink buttressed pieces
with crisp mold: vase (856-8″) with peppering throughout and flowerpot (64-5″) without under plate (minor flake to corner of one buttress), impressed marks.
$150-$200/pair

Two Ixia pink vases
one with collared rim (illegible mark) and one flaring (852-6″), both have crisp molds, impressed marks; taller: 10 1/2″ by 4 3/4″.
$275-$325/pair

Two Ixia yellow pieces
basket (846-10″) with soft mold and restoration to handle and pillow vase (858-8″), rim has two glaze scales, 1/2″ and 1/4″, and a small flake, impressed marks.
$250-$275/pair

Ixia yellow console set
consisting of a circular center bowl (329-7″) and a pair of buttressed candlesticks (1126-4 1/4″), impressed marks.
$175-$200/set

Two Ixia yellow pieces
small planter (illegible mark) and footed vase with two buttressed supports (861-10″), impressed marks; planter: 4 1/2″ by 4 1/2″.
$300-$350/pair

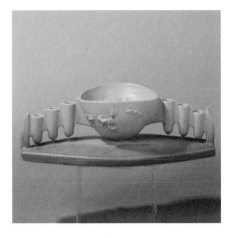

Ixia yellow combination planter and candlestick holder
(328) with minor flecks to rim and base, impressed mark, 4 1/4″ by 12 1/4″.
$250-$300

Two Ixia yellow vases
one flaring (854-7″) and one ovoid (853-6″), one minute burst to each, impressed marks.
$375-$400/pair

Jonquil

Introduced about 1931, Jonquil has trios of flowers girdling a textured body that has a color transition of mottled brown and ivory moving up to muddy brown and green. The interiors are usually glazed in a brighter variegated green. Pieces are unmarked with silver foil labels.

Jonquil basket
paper label, rare, 8 1/2″ by 5 1/2″.

$350-$450

Jonquil flaring center bowl
with built-in flower frog, strong mold, unmarked, rare, 10 1/2″ diameter.

$400-$500

Pair of Jonquil candlesticks
unmarked, 4 1/4″ tall each.

$650-$750/pair

Jonquil console set
stilt-pull chip to bowl, silver foil label on candlesticks; candlesticks: 4 1/4″ by 4 1/4″; bowl: 3 3/4″ by 12″.

$500-$600

Jonquil jardinière
spider lines to base (lines go through), minor nicks to high points, unmarked, 9″ by 11″.

$275-$325

Jonquil jardinière
several nicks overall, 3/4″ chip to one handle, unmarked, 9″ by 12 1/2″.

$225-$275

Jonquil strawberry planter
with attached under plate, unmarked, rare, 6 1/4″ by 8 1/2″.

$800-$900

Jonquil bulbous vase
nick to one flower, unmarked, 6 1/4″ by 5 3/4″.
$200-$250

Jonquil bulbous vase
with crisp mold, professionally restored 1/2″ chip
at rim, some minor nicks at base, unmarked,
12 1/4″ tall.
$450-$550

Jonquil bulbous handled vase
unmarked, 8″ by 6 7/8″ by 6 7/8″.
$550-$650

Jonquil bulbous vase
unmarked, 6 3/4″ by 7 1/4″.
$225-$275

Jonquil bulbous vase
2″ line from rim, unmarked, 4 1/4″ by 6 1/4″.
$125-$175

Jonquil bulbous vase
with crisp mold, unmarked, 6″ by 7″.
$250-$300

Jonquil bulbous vase
unmarked, 8 1/4″ by 7 1/4″.
$300-$375

Jonquil flaring vase
black paper label, 7 1/4″ by 4 1/2″.

$300-$375

Jonquil gourd-shaped vase
bruise to one flower, pinhead-sized fleck to rim, unmarked, 8 1/4″ by 5 1/2″.

$325-$375

Jonquil bulbous vase
with flaring rim, burst bubbles to base, unmarked, 9 1/2″ by 6 1/4″.

$350-$400

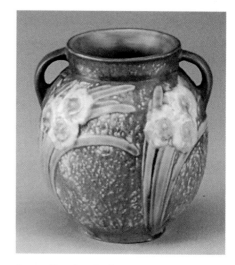

Two Jonquil pieces
spherical vase and oval center bowl, unmarked, 4″ tall and 4 1/4″ tall.

$325-$375/pair

Jonquil spherical vase
unmarked, 5″ tall.

$225-$275

Jonquil flaring vase
unmarked, 7″ by 5″.

$175-$225

Jonquil squat vessel
small stilt-pull chips, unmarked, 4″ by 4 1/2″.

$125-$175

Jonquil flaring wall pocket
silver foil tag, 8″ tall.

$650-$750

Juvenile

Considered part of the creamwares, the Juvenile pieces have bright bands of color and transfer decorations of playful animals and children. There is also a rare Santa Claus motif. Most pieces are unmarked, but occasionally have an "Rv" ink stamp.

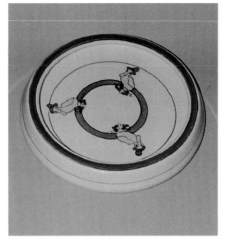

Juvenile dish
with duck in boots and hat, some losses to enamel, "Rv" ink stamp, 7 3/4″ diameter.

$65-$75

Juvenile dish and cup
decorated with rabbits, ("ears down"), several minor nicks overall, "Rv" ink stamp to both; bowl: 8″ diameter.

$175-$225/pair

Two Juvenile pieces
bowl with girls in bonnets (several chips to rim) and mug with ducks (hairline to rim), "Rv" ink stamps to both; bowl: 5 1/4″ diameter.

$80-$100/pair

Juvenile mug
decorated with rabbits, ("ears up"), minute fleck, several bruises (in firing), hairline, unmarked, 3″ by 3 3/4″.

$110-$140

Three-piece Juvenile set
decorated with chicks: cup, saucer, and small plate, some light wear to decoration, unmarked; plate: 6 1/2″ diameter.

$225-$275/set

Three-piece Juvenile set
decorated with rabbits ("ears down") and a green stripe, consisting of a cereal bowl (No. 13), creamer (No. 13), and sugar (No. 6), "Rv" ink stamps, bowl: 6″ diameter.

$900-$1,000/set

La Rose

Introduced in 1924, La Rose features evenly spaced garland swags and clusters of roses and leaves on a creamy background. Pieces are unmarked or have an "Rv" ink stamp.

Three La Rose vessels
low bowl with crisp mold and burst clay bubbles, double bud vase, and ovoid vase with 1/2" bruise to rim; two have "Rv" ink stamp; bowl: 9" diameter; vases: 4 1/4" by 9", and 6 1/4" tall.
$300-$350/set

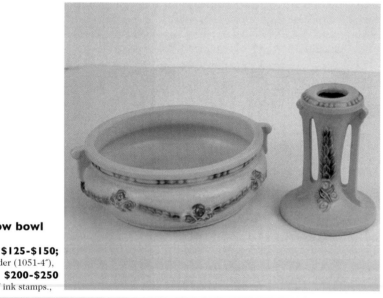

La Rose low bowl
(127-7"),
$125-$150;
and candleholder (1051-4"),
$200-$250
both with "Rv" ink stamps.,

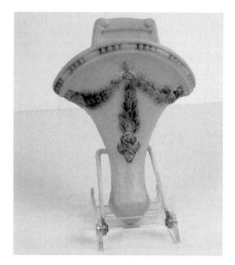

La Rose wall pocket
(1233-7"), "Rv" ink stamp.
$400-$450

Landscape

Part of the creamwares made about 1915, this decoration is frequently found on tea sets, and pots for coffee or chocolate. It may also picture a woodland stream in brown or blue on white. These pieces are unmarked, and are often heavily crazed.

Landscape teapot
creamer, and sugar set with transfer seascapes in blue.
$300-$350

Laurel

A mix of nature and art deco, Laurel (1934) features tapering leaves and berries draped over panels of three vertical grooves. Dripping glazes cover bodies of ochre, mottled orange-red, and dusty green, but other color combinations continue to be found. Pieces are unmarked or have gold foil labels.

Trial glaze Laurel vase
with two low buttressed handles, covered in a dark brown and rich amber glaze, gold foil label, 12 1/4˝ by 8˝.
$1,100

Laurel green bulbous vase
with collared rim, unmarked, 6˝ by 3 3/4˝.
$275-$325

Laurel green vessel
with abrasion around rim and flake to rib, unmarked, 6 1/2˝ by 7˝.
$225-$275

Laurel red vase
with buttressed handles, nick and 1/2˝ chip to base, gold foil label, 8˝ by 6 1/2˝.
$110-$140

Laurel red vase
with buttressed handles, foil label, and remnant of store label, 7 1/2˝ by 5˝.
$225-$275

Laurel yellow console set
center bowl and a pair of candlesticks, line to one candlestick, chips to the other, foil label on one; bowl: 4˝ by 9 1/2˝.
$300-$350/set

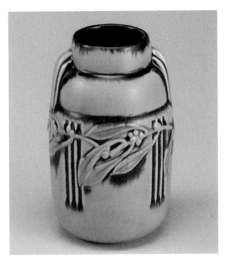

Laurel yellow ovoid vase
unmarked, 6˝ by 3 1/2˝.
$200-$250

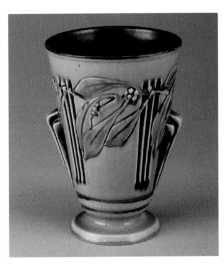

Laurel yellow flaring vase
unmarked, 10 1/4˝ tall.
$450-$500

Lotus

Introduced near the end of the company's existence in 1951, Lotus features a tight "picket fence" of leaves, usually in ivory or yellow, banded on the top and bottom by colors that included blue, green, red, brown, and yellow. Pieces are distinctly marked with "Lotus" and a style number/size.

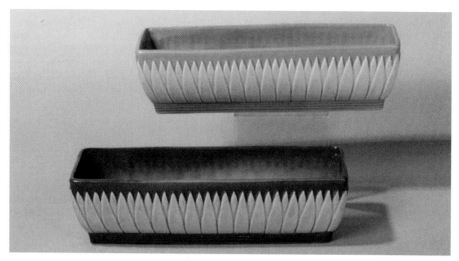

Two Lotus rectangular planters
one green and one blue (L7-10 1/2"), raised marks
$350-$400/pair

Two Lotus vases
(L3-10"), one in blue and ivory, the other in green and yellow, raised marks.
$250-$300/ pair

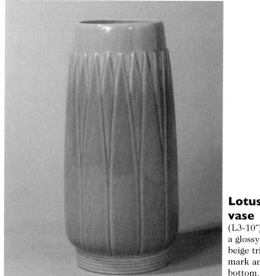

Lotus tapering vase
(L3-10") covered in a glossy sky blue and beige trial glaze, raised mark and glaze codes to bottom.
$800-$900

Two Lotus pieces
one red vase (L3-10") and a square brown planter (L9-4") with minor firing bruise to one corner of base, raised marks.
$150-$200/ pair

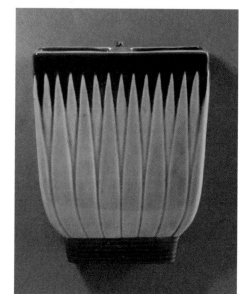

Lotus green wall pocket
(L8-7") with a very short inner firing line, raised mark.
$550-$600

Lombardy

The bulbous reeded design of Lombardy was introduced in 1924. The finish can be dull or glossy, and the colors are mostly solid blues and greens. Pieces are unmarked.

Lombardy blue-green hanging basket
with abrasion to bottom, unmarked, 6 1/4″ wide.
$100-$125

Lombardy dark green hanging basket
with abrasion to bottom, unmarked, 7 3/4″ wide.
$150-$200

Two Lombardy pieces
green small dish with bruise to rim, and blue vase, black paper label on one, 2″ by 5 1/2″ and 6 1/2″ by 4″.
$90-$110/pair

Lombardy wall pocket
covered in a blue-gray glossy glaze, unmarked, 9″ tall.
$250-$300

Lombardy wall pocket
in a gray-blue matte glaze, unmarked, 9 1/2″ tall.
$250-$300

Luffa

From 1934, Luffa features small yellow or white flowers and large green leaves on a wavy ridged surface. Background colors are dominant green with brown accents, or dominant brown with variegated green accents. Pieces are unmarked or have foil labels.

Luffa brown console set
consisting of a four-sided center bowl with scalloped rim (underglaze bruise to rim) and a pair of short candlesticks (good mold, one has small fleck and touch-up to 1/4″ rim chip, other has minor burst bubble to rim), unmarked; bowl: 3 3/4″ by 13 1/4″, sticks: 5″ tall.
$225-$275/set

Luffa brown bulbous jardinière
2″ hairline from rim, unmarked, 6 1/2″ by 6 1/2″.
$150-$200

Luffa brown planter
unmarked, 5″ by 7″.
$150-$200

Two Luffa pieces
brown rectangular footed bowl and green tapering vase, unmarked; 4 1/4″ by 9 1/2″ and 6 1/2″ by 4 1/2″.
$250-$300/pair

Luffa green bowl
unmarked, 4″ by 10″.
$275-$325

Two Luffa brown vases
one with collared rim, the other cylindrical, unmarked, 6 1/4″ and 6 1/2″ tall.
$275-$325/pair

Two Luffa pieces
green planter with small repaired chips to base and brown bulbous vase with small nick to base, foil label on planter; 5″ and 6″ tall.

$325-$375/pair

Two Luffa vases
one brown ovoid (good mold, 2″ hairline from rim) and one green with flaring rim (1/2″ bruise to rim), unmarked; 7 1/2″ by 4 1/2″ and 7 1/4″ by 4 3/4″.
$275-$325/pair

Luffa green ovoid vase
with collared rim, some peppering to rim and
bruise to base, unmarked, 8 1/4″ by 5 1/4″.
$175-$225

Luffa green tapering vase
unmarked, 6″ by 4″.
$175-$225

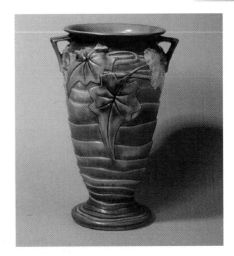

Luffa green tapering footed vase
strong mold and good color, unmarked, 14 1/2″ by
9 3/4″.
$750-$850

Two Luffa green vases
each with collared rim (one is sea foam green, the
other emerald green), unmarked, 6 1/4″ by 3 3/4″
each.
$400-$450/pair

Luffa green bulbous vessel
unmarked, 6 1/2″ by 6 1/2″.
$400-$450

Luffa green wall pocket
unmarked, 8 1/4″.
$650-$750

Lustre

Introduced in 1921 or '22, Lustre also
borrowed from Rosecraft shapes and
offered the high-gloss colors of azure,
blue, pink, orange, and yellow. Pieces
are unmarked or have a paper label.

Three tall Lustre candlesticks
pair of orange (one minor fleck to each, a few
insignificant color scratches, one has short line to
base) and single ivory (shallow 2″ hairline to base),
all unmarked, each approximately 10″ tall.
$150-$200/set

Two Lustre baskets in glossy pink
left, 297, 7 1/2″, unmarked.
$300-$350;

right, 299, 9″, black paper label.
$350-$400

Magnolia

Though the magnolia is the most ancient of flowering plants, Roseville didn't introduce this line until very late in its existence-1943. It's also not clear what species this is (there are about 75), since magnolias typically have a single center receptacle, and the pottery flowers appear to have several. The large blooms on gnarled black branches can be found on backgrounds of blue with brown and amber-green accents, orange-brown with green accents, and green with brown-yellow accents. Pieces feature raised marks.

Experimental Magnolia blue bulbous urn
with the inscription "Magnolia Blossoms/White Flowers/Green or Pink Centers/Branches Dark Brown" on reverse, otherwise unmarked, 9" by 8 1/2".

$3,500

Magnolia blue cookie jar
(2-8"), a couple of small chips, bruises, and burst bubbles, raised mark.

$125-$175

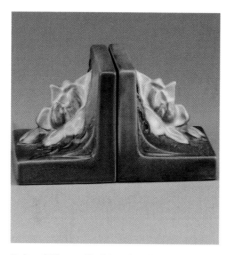

Pair of Magnolia blue bookends
(13), restoration to one corner, 5 1/4" by 5 1/4" by 5 3/4".

$110-$140/pair

Magnolia blue ewer
(15-15"), minor peppering overall and 1/2" glaze miss to base, raised mark.

$300-$350

Five Magnolia blue pieces
water pitcher with cracked handle, large vase with chips, ewer with reglued spout, single low candlestick, and rectangular planter, all marked.

$225-$275/set

Six Magnolia pieces
blue cornucopia vase (184-6"), brown bowl (448-8"), pair of blue candlesticks (1157-4 1/2"), blue sugar dish (4-S), and brown rectangular planter (389-8"), raised marks.

$275-$325/set

Three Magnolia pieces
pair of blue vases (87-6″), one with nick to base, and
vase (92-8″) with nick to one branch, all marked.

$175-$225/set

Magnolia blue bulbous vase
(96-12″), raised mark.

$110-$140

Three Magnolia brown pieces
shell-shaped planter, basket planter, and bulbous
vase (small chips), all marked; tallest: 8″

$200-$250/set

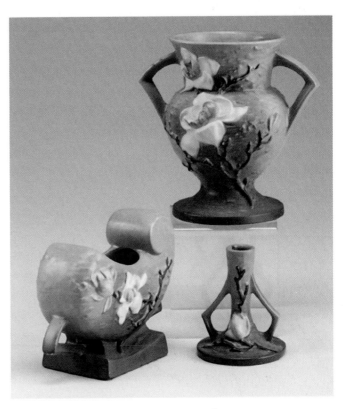

Three Magnolia brown pieces
planter (183-6″), candlestick (1157-4 1/2″), and
vase (181-8″) with restoration to base, all marked.

$150-$200/set

Magnolia blue squat vessel
faint raised mark, 5 3/8″ by 3 1/4″ by 4 5/8″.
$70-$80

Magnolia brown bud vase
(179-7″), raised mark, 7 3/8″ by 5 1/8″.
$150-$200

Magnolia brown cornucopia vase
(184-6″), raised mark, 6″ by 6 5/8″ by 6 1/4″.
$125-$150

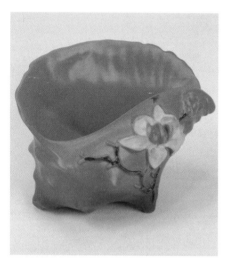

Magnolia conch shell planter
(454-8″), raised mark, 9 1/2″ by 6 3/8″ by 6 1/4″.
$200-$250

Magnolia green basket
(385-10″), raised mark, base chips, 12 1/2″ by
9 7/8″ by 6 1/2″.
$150-$200

Magnolia green cookie jar
(2-8″), raised mark, 8 3/4″ by 10 1/2″.
$575-$625

Magnolia green creamer
(4-C) and sugar (4-S); creamer: 5 3/8″ by 3 1/4″ by 4 1/2″; sugar: 5 3/8″ by 5 3/4″ by 2 3/8″.
$150-$200/pair

Magnolia green teapot
(4), raised mark, 7 3/4″ by 8″ by 10″.
$350-$400

Magnolia green double bud vase
(186-4 1/2″), 9″ by 4 7/8″ by 2 7/8″.

$175-$225

Magnolia green tea set
(4) with small underglaze bruise and underglaze chip inside, and hairlines to base of teapot, and small burst bubble inside rim of creamer, raised marks; teapot: 7″ by 10 1/2″.

$150-$200/set

Magnolia green two-handled vase
(89-7″), 7 1/4″ by 5 1/4″ by 3 3/8″.

$175-$225

Magnolia green two-handled flaring vase
(88-6″), raised mark, 6 1/4″ by 5 3/8″ by 3 1/4″.

$125-$150

Two Magnolia green pieces

bulbous vase with chip to flower and Magnolia bowl (448-8˝) with fleck to one handle and chip to tip of flower at rim, raised marks.

$110-$140/pair

Three Magnolia green pieces

cornucopia vase (184-6˝) with small chip to petal, flowerpot (666-5˝) with hairline and flakes, and center bowl (449-10˝) with small chips, all marked.

$125-$165/set

Mara

An iridescent line in the Rozane Wares meant to compete with Weller's Sicardo (also spelled Sicard), Mara (circa 1904) came in forms first created by Roseville a decade earlier. Pieces are rarely marked with a wafer.

Courtesy Adamstown Antique Gallery

Mara vase

(K-22) with contrasting scroll design on a glossy raspberry glaze, faint impressed mark, 8 1/2˝ tall.

$500-$600

Mara bulbous tapering vase

unmarked, 8˝ by 5˝.

$3,500-$3,700

Mara tapering vase

with sprays of flowers and leaves, 2˝ tight hairline to rim, unmarked, 7 3/4˝ by 2 1/2˝.

$300-$400

Matt Color

This line was introduced about 1920 and featured simple designs, often ribbed, fluted, or with recessed panels. Pieces are unmarked or have foil labels.

Four Matt Color squat vessels
in gold, green, blue-green, and royal blue, one has silver foil label, each measures 4˝ by 7˝.

$150-$200/set

Matt Color two-handled planter
unmarked, 3 3/4˝ by 6˝.

$60-$80

Five Matt Color vessels
two spherical and three bulbous, in assorted glazes, unmarked, 3 3/4˝ by 5 1/2˝ and 4˝ by 5 3/4˝.

$200-$250/set

Four Matt Color pieces
two vases, one pink and one blue, and two beehive-shaped vessels with short loop handles, one in blue and one in gold; some small burst bubbles; one has foil label; largest: 6 1/4˝ by 4 1/4˝.

$150-$200/set

Three Matt Color pieces
green and blue hanging basket (bruise to rim of one, glaze flake to other) and blue bowl; two marked; baskets: 4 1/2˝ by 6 1/2˝.

$110-$140/set

Matt Green

Its name says it all. Introduced about 1910, there were more than 100 styles, mostly planters, jardinières, pedestals, vases, and bowls, both plain and embossed, but they're not easy to find. Pieces are unmarked or have paper labels.

Matt Green footed planter
unmarked, 9˝ by 10 1/2˝.

$400-$450

Two Matt Green pieces
a flaring vase (shape 5), impressed mark, 9˝ tall, $350-$400; and a flower frog bowl, unmarked, 2 1/2˝ tall.

$150-$200

Matt Green umbrella stand
(727 B), unmarked, 20 3/8˝ tall.

$1,200-$1,500

Mayfair

Introduced in the late 1940s, this glossy, colorful line came in both stylized and natural floral motifs on vases, pots, planters, and pitchers. Pieces have raised marks.

Mayfair basket
in glossy brown with tan interior (1012-10˝), raised mark, 8 1/2˝ by 10˝.

$150-$175

Two Mayfair tankard-form pitchers
(1107-12˝), one green and one brown, both embossed with ferns, raised marks.

$150-$200/pair

Ming Tree

Although the decoration on this line has been described as a Japanese bonsai tree, "Ming" was one of the Chinese dynasties. Maybe Roseville was trying to cover all the bases with this 1949 introduction. On bodies of glossy Celestial Blue, Jade Green and Temple White, these pieces also have gnarled branches for handles. Pieces have the raised mark, "Roseville U.S.A."

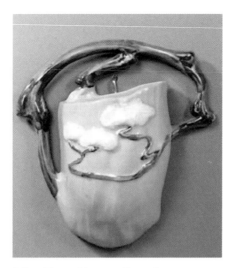

Ming Tree blue wall pocket
(566-8″), raised mark.

$150-$200

Ming Tree blue vase
(510-14″), small flat chip to bottom, raised mark.

$150-$200

Four Ming Tree pieces
two ashtrays (599), one blue and one green (small bruise to rim of blue one), blue planter (526-9″), and white vase (582-8″) with reglued handle, raised marks.

$125-$175/set

Three Ming Tree blue pieces
pair of low candlesticks (551) and a tall basket vase (510-14″) with restoration to rim, raised marks.

$150-$200/set

Three Ming Tree blue pieces
pair of bookends (559) with abrasion to back, and tall vase (583-10″) with small chips to bottom, raised marks.

$150-$200/pair

Two Ming Tree green pieces
pitcher (516-10″) and two-handled vase (582-8″), raised marks.

$250-$300/pair

Ming Tree green floor vase
(586-15″), raised mark.

$700-$800

Three Ming Tree pieces
tall basket vase (510-14″) in ivory with restored crack at base and pair of blue bookends (559), raised marks.

$350-$450/set

Mock Orange

A throwback to the designs of the 1930s, Mock Orange (1950) featured delicate tiny blossoms on slender stalks, with backgrounds commonly in green, pink, or yellow. The raised mark of "Roseville U.S.A." also included "Mock Orange," or it had a foil label.

Mock Orange green footed basket
(910-10˝), restoration where rim and handle meet on one side, raised mark.

$300-$350

Mock Orange green floor vase
(986-18˝) with ruffled rim, raised mark.

$550-$650

Mock Orange green four-piece coffee and tea set
(971), 1/2˝ chip and small bruise under rim of one lid and 1/2˝ chip to edge of teapot, also has minor spider lines to spout; coffee pot has a 3˝ hairline, raised marks; coffee pot: 10 3/4˝ by 7 1/2˝.

$300-$350/set

Three Mock Orange pieces
green jardinière (900-4˝) and two vases (984-10˝), one green and one yellow, raised marks.

$500-$550/set

Mock Orange pink square pillow vase
(92-7˝), minor flat chip to one foot, raised mark, 7 1/4˝ by 7 1/4˝.

$125-$175

Mock Orange pink vase
(985-12˝) with squat base and flaring rim, repair to 1˝ section of rim, raised mark.

$125-$175

Mock Orange yellow hanging basket
1/4˝ glaze inconsistency to rim, stamped "U.S.A.," 5 1/2˝ by 7 1/4˝.

$250-$300

Mock Orange yellow coffee/tea set
(971-T, 971-S, 971-C, 971-P), repair to chip on lid of coffee pot, raised marks.
$750-$850/set

Two Mock Orange yellow pieces
footed bowl (927-6˝) and vase (982-8˝), raised marks.
$150-$200/pair

Mock Orange yellow ewer
(918-16˝), raised mark.
$550-$650

Mock Orange yellow jardinière
(902-8˝) and pedestal (905-8˝), 1/4˝ flake to one handle of jardinière, some small pockmarks to base of pedestal, raised marks.
$700-$800

Four Mock Orange yellow pieces
fan vase (921-6˝), ewer (916-6˝), jardinière (941-6˝), and vase (983-7˝), raised marks.
$400-$500/set

Three Mock Orange yellow planters
(969-12˝), (968-8˝), and (982-7˝), raised marks.
$300-$350/set

Three Mock Orange planters
yellow (933-11˝), green (934-12˝), and pink (911-8˝), raised marks.
$300-$350/set

Moderne

Introduced at the height of art deco, Moderne (1936) picked up and refined themes introduced two years earlier in Laurel: strong vertical lines juxtaposed with stylized blossoms or tendrils. The plain matt backgrounds include blue, brown, pink, green, and ivory. Most pieces have impressed marks.

Moderne blue triple candlestick
(1112), line through base, marked, 6″ tall.
$150-$200

Two Moderne pieces
blue urn and beige footed vase (796-8″) with underglaze chip below rim, raised mark to one.
$200-$250/pair

Moderne green chalice
(789-6″), impressed mark.
$125-$175

Two Moderne green vases
bud (790-7″) with fleck to body, and ovoid (797-8″), impressed marks; bud vase also has foil label.
$200-$250/pair

Moderne white footed vase
(803-14″), restoration to hairline at base, impressed mark.
$250-$300

Moderne blue console set
consisting of an oval center bowl (301-10″) and pair of candlesticks (1111-4 1/2″), impressed marks.

$300-$350/set

Two Moderne blue vases
one (802-12″) with several chips to base and one to rim, and a tall one with squat base (800-10″) with small chip to bottom ring and fleck to corner, impressed marks.

$650-$750/pair

Two Moderne pieces
blue urn (787-6″) and rust flaring basket, one marked; bowl: 8″ diameter.

$325-$375/pair

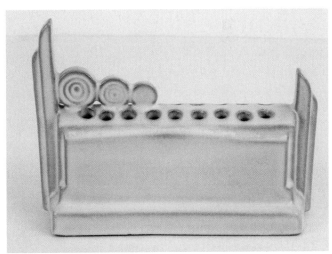

Moderne white flower frog
(27), impressed mark, 6 1/2″ wide by 5″ tall.

$225-$250

Two Moderne white coupe-shaped vases
(788-6″ and 787-6″), impressed marks and foil label to one.

$250-$300/pair

Three Moderne white pieces
bud vase (790-7″) and a pair of triple candlesticks (1112) with hairline to base of one and restoration to rim chip on other, impressed marks; candlesticks: 6 1/4″ tall.

$200-$250/set

Mongol

The glaze that has come to be known as Mongol first received wide recognition in 1904 when the line won first prize at the St. Louis Centennial Exposition. Called oxblood or "sang de boeuf," the blood-red glossy glaze was part of the Rozane line. It would turn other colors if refired, and some pieces have been found with hand-painted decoration, and with silver or gold overlay. Some have a Rozane Ware/ Mongol wafer, or paper labels.

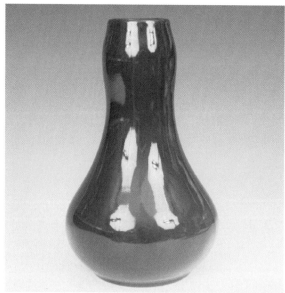

Mongol vase
in a Mara shape (K-22), Rozane Ware wafer, 8″ tall.

$550-$650

Montacello

Sometimes misspelled Monticello, this line from 1931 has a Southwestern flavor. A collar of watery brown, tan-pink, and green is accented with a modified fleur-de-lis (on some almost an arrowhead shape) in ivory that drips across evenly spaced black ovals. Backgrounds of these heavy-bodied pieces are mottled blue, brown, and green. Pieces are unmarked, or rarely have a silver or black label.

Montacello blue console set
consisting of a faceted center bowl and a pair of candlesticks, very good mold, unmarked; bowl: 3″ by 13 1/4″, sticks: 5″ tall.

$800-$900/set

Montacello blue ovoid vase
unmarked, 7 1/4″ by 5 3/4″.

$500-$550

Montacello blue bulbous vessel
unmarked, 7 1/4″ by 6 1/4″.

$550-$650

Two Montacello blue pieces
vase with flaring rim (1/4″ chip to rim) and corseted vessel, both unmarked, 5 1/2″ by 5″ and 4 1/4″ by 5 1/2″.

$300-$350/pair

Montacello bulbous vase
covered in an unusual mottled blue glaze,
unmarked, 7 1/2″ by 6 1/2″.

$600-$700

Montacello brown two-handled vase
with white fleur-de-lis, unmarked, 4 1/4″ by 5″.

$300-$350

Montacello brown bulbous vessel
unmarked, 6 1/4″ by 7 1/4″.

450-$500

Montacello brown squat basket
with arched handle, unmarked, 6 1/2″ by 4 3/4″.

$700-$800

Two Montacello brown pieces
bulbous vase with flaring rim and corseted vessel,
both unmarked, 5 1/4″ by 4 1/2″ and 4 1/4″ by 5″.

$400-$450/pair

Montacello brown tapering vase
unmarked, 7 1/4″ by 5 1/2″.

$450-$550

Two Montacello brown vessels
one with flaring rim and one bulbous, unmarked,
5 1/4″ by 5″ and 5″ by 5 3/4″.

$600-$700/pair

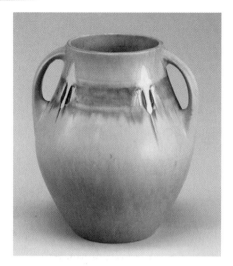

Montacello green vase
unmarked, 9 1/2″ by 8″.
$800-$900

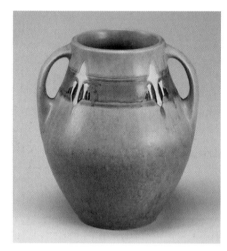

Montacello green vase
restoration inside rim and to base, firing line to
one handle, light abrasion, unmarked, 9″ by 8 1/4″.
$350-$400

Montacello green bulbous vase
unmarked, 7 1/2″ by 6″.
$450-$500

Montacello green flaring vase
bruise and 1/2″ colored-in chip to rim, unmarked,
11″ by 6″.
$525-$575

**Montacello green two-handled
corseted vessel**
peppering to one side, a couple of small glaze
misses to rim, unmarked, 5″ tall.
$175-$225

Two Montacello vases in mottled glazes
the vase on the left (560) has a turquoise band, 6 1/4″ tall,
$550-$650;
on right (557), the mottled blue glaze also has a brown band trimmed in blue,
5″ tall.
$400-$450

Morning Glory

Introduced in 1935, the appearance of Morning Glory—a looping tangle of flowers, vines, and leaves—owes much to some of the stylized floral patterns found on Ceramic Design pieces of three decades earlier. The lavender, yellow, and pale green palette with dark accents on an ivory or green body is quite distinctive. Pieces are unmarked or feature foil labels.

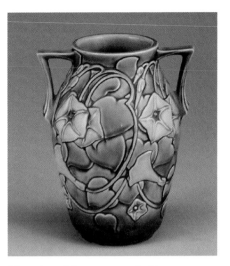

Morning Glory green bulbous vase
unmarked, 8 1/2″ by 6 1/2″.

$900-$1,100

Pair of Morning Glory green candlesticks
minor bruise to base of one, foil label, 5″ by 4 1/4″.

$450-$500/pair

Morning Glory green oblong planter
unmarked, 4 3/4″ by 11″.

$450-$500

Morning Glory white oblong planter
strong mold and good color, unmarked, 5″ by 13″.

$350-$400

Morning Glory green flaring vase
with strong mold and good color, restoration to flat chip under foot ring, unmarked, 14 3/4″ by 10″.

$1,800-$2,000

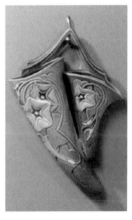

Morning Glory green double wall pocket
light glaze scaling (from firing) to tip of shorter holder, unmarked, 8 1/2″.

$850-$950

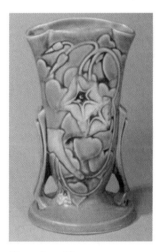

Morning Glory green flaring pillow vase
foil label, 7 1/4″ by 4″.

$450-$500

Morning Glory white flaring vase
small chip to rim, unmarked, 8 1/4″ by 6 3/4″.

$300-$350

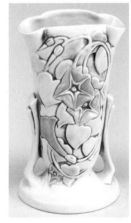

Morning Glory white flaring pillow vase
foil label, 7″ by 4 3/4″.

$300-$350

Morning Glory white vase
nick and several restorations, unmarked, 6 1/2″ by 4 1/4″.

$150-$200

Morning Glory white pear-shaped vase
1″ tight hairline to rim, grinding chips to base, foil label, 10 1/4″ by 7″.

$300-$350

Moss

Another introduction from 1936, Moss evokes the bayou country, with dripping brown glaze hanging from long-leafed branches. Backgrounds include blue, blue-green, tan-brown, and pink-turquoise. Most pieces feature impressed marks.

Moss pink console bowl
(293-10″) with some peppering, impressed mark.
$100-$150

Moss blue bulbous vase
(783-9″), impressed mark.

$350-$400

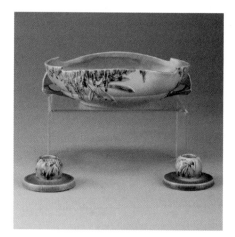

Moss blue vase
lines to rim, several small chips to base (some touched up), unmarked, 14 1/2″ tall.

$275-$325

Moss blue console set
consisting of a bowl (293-10″) and a pair of low candlesticks (1109) with a couple of chips to one, all marked.

$250-$300/set

Moss pink pillow vase
(778-7″), impressed mark.

$250-$300

Moss green bulbous vase
(783-9″), very crisp mold and good color, impressed mark.

$300-$350

Moss blue flowerpot
(637-5″) and under plate, good mold and brilliant color, impressed mark.

$250-$300

Two Moss urns
(779-8˝ and 776-7˝), chip to base and rim of smaller, chips to restored base of larger, both marked.

$375-$425/pair

Two Moss pieces
blue urn and pink planter (small burst to one handle), both unmarked, 8 1/2˝ and 4 1/4˝ tall.

$375-$425/pair

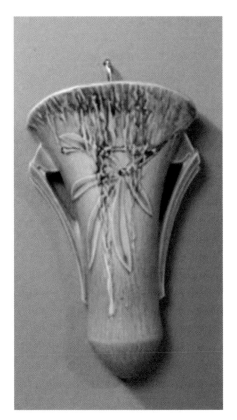

Moss blue wall pocket
(278-8˝), firing line inside one handle, raised mark.

$400-$450

Moss pink ovoid vase
(786-14˝) with crisp mold and bright color, 1˝ chip and another restored chip to base, 2˝ tight line from rim (only goes through at the top), and two small nicks to leaf, impressed mark.

$550-$650

Moss pink bucket wall pocket
1/2˝ chip to bottom tip and small nick to edge, unmarked, 10˝ tall.

$400-$500

Mostique

Dating from about 1915, Mostique is probably the most common Roseville pattern after Pine Cone, with about 80 different styles known. Crudely stylized leaf and floral patterns, often in spade shapes, alternate with heavy lines and geometric forms on textured bodies of gray or tan. Most pieces are unmarked.

Two Mostique pieces
hanging basket with spade-shaped blossoms (nicks and abrasions) and planter with Glasgow roses; a few glaze flakes overall, "Rv" ink stamp to one; planter: 9" by 10 1/2".

$275-$325/pair

Mostique bowl
"R" ink stamp, 6 3/4" by 2 7/8".

$60-$80

Mostique jardinière
with Glasgow roses, some nicks to high points, unmarked, 9 1/2" tall.

$110-$140

Mostique jardinière
with Glasgow roses and spade-shaped leaves in polychrome, a few nicks, unmarked, 9" by 11".

$125-$175

Mostique jardinière and pedestal
one line and a couple of very minor nicks to jardinière, two small chips and lines to base of pedestal, unmarked; jardinière: 10" tall, pedestal: 18" tall.

$750-$850

Mostique pedestal
covered in unusual glossy green to amber glaze, restoration to base, chip to top, unmarked, 18" by 11 1/2".

$175-$225

Three Mostique pieces
two planters and corseted vase, a couple of small chips to each, unmarked; tallest: 10".

$150-$200/set

Four Mostique pieces
two corseted vases with spade-shaped leaves and
two low bowls; hairlines to large bowl, nicks to all,
and 1/2″ chip to smaller vase, some stamped "Rv";
tallest:
8″.

$225-$275/set

Three Mostique pieces
two corseted vases and bowl, all decorated with
yellow spade-shaped leaves; bowl in as-is condition
(chips/cracks), bruise to base of large vase, and
glaze chips to all three; each is marked with
impressed numbers; vases, 8″ tall, 10 1/2″ tall,
8 3/4″ diameter.

$200-$250/set

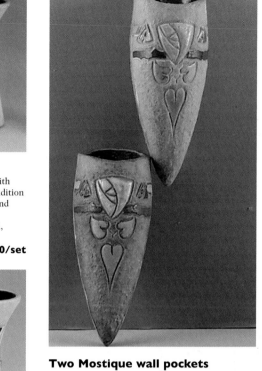

Two Mostique wall pockets
some scaling and nicks to high points, unmarked,
10″.

$350-$400/pair

Two Mostique pieces
corseted vase and bowl, unmarked, 6″ tall and 7″
diameter.

$125-$175/pair

Two Mostique vases
with spade-shaped flowers, unmarked, 10″ and 12″.

$325-$375/pair

Two Mostique vases
one cylindrical with Glasgow rose (opposing lines,
fleck to rim), the other bulbous with papyrus
(small flecks), unmarked, 10″ and 8″ tall.

$325-$375/pair

Mostique vase
"Rv" ink stamp, 10″ by 5 1/4″.

$175-$225

Mostique wall pocket
oval with stylized dogwood (two minor glaze nicks
to hole), unmarked, 9 1/2″ tall.

$350-$450

Normandy

Closely related to Donatello and Corinthian, Normandy (mid-1920s) features a similar color scheme and overall profile, but has a banded tangle of stylized grapevines on a terracotta background. Pieces often have an "Rv" ink stamp.

Normandy hanging basket
with good mold and color, "Rv" ink stamp, 7" tall.

$275-$325

Normandy jardinière
with chip and drill-hole to base, unmarked, 8" by 9 1/2".

$125-$175

Normandy jardinière
restoration to rim chip and 1" firing line to base, unmarked, 9" by 11".

$90-$110

Normandy jardinière
small chip to decoration, "Rv" ink stamp, 10" by 12".

$150 to $200

Normandy umbrella stand
several small flakes to ribs, bruise and hairlines to base, blue ink stamp, 20" by 10".

$375-$425

Nursery

Also part of the creamwares, but not to be confused with the Juvenile line, Nursery pieces, circa 1912, have broad rims on low bowls that were suited for feeding in a high chair. They are transfer decorated with about a dozen rhymes, but are otherwise unmarked.

Nursery "Baby's Plate"
with Little Bo Peep rhyme, unmarked, 7 3/4" diameter.

$200-$250

Olympic

Part of the Rozane Wares, Olympic (1905) features transfer images of ancient Greece on a red background and are usually titled. Pieces are sometimes artist signed or marked "Rozane Olympic."

Olympic pitcher
"Ulysses at the Table of Circe," restoration to 5″ spider lines from rim, half of the pitcher is overpainted, signed and titled, 7″ by 8 1/2″.
$1,300-$1,400

Rozane Olympic vase
double handled pedestal form, painted mark, "Euryclea discovers Ulysses," 11″ tall, minor glaze scratches, restored.
$1,800-$2,200

Olympic vase
marked on the bottom, "Rozane Olympic Pottery–Minerva, Hector and Mercury" and shape number 56, 12″ tall.
$4,000-$5,000

Orian

Sometimes misspelled "Orion," this line from 1935 is not a typical art deco motif. The delicate, sinuous handles are more related to art nouveau. The vivid colors include blue, yellow, green, red, peach, and pink with softer accents, and the interiors are frequently a stark contrast: mint with raspberry or turquoise with brown. Pieces can have raised or impressed marks, foil labels, or be unmarked.

Pair of Orian vases
with squat base, in blue and brown, unmarked, 7 1/2″ by 5″ each.
$275-$325/pair

Two Orian pieces
oval center bowl in brown and green (272-10″) with minor grinding chips and vase in raspberry and blue, raised mark and foil label, 7 1/4″ by 4″ each.
$300-$350/pair

Pair of Orian footed vases
(733-6˝), one yellow and green, one blue and
brown with glaze bubbles to body, raised marks.
$200-$225/pair

Orian brown vase
with squat stepped base, mint green interior,
unmarked, 7˝ by 8˝.
$200-$225

Orian blue double wall pocket
minor flake at hanging point, silver foil label,
8 1/4˝ by 4˝.
$750-$850

Orian salmon pink vase
with squat base and stovepipe neck, unmarked, 6
1/2˝ by 8 1/2˝.
$125-$175

Orian peach bowl
(272-10˝) with turquoise interior, impressed mark.
$175-$225

Orian classically shaped vase
with two buttressed handles, the exterior in glossy
raspberry, the interior in mint green, unmarked,
11˝ by 4˝.
$250-$300

Orian oval footed bowl
with raspberry exterior and mint green interior, unmarked, 4″ by 10 1/2″.

$175-$225

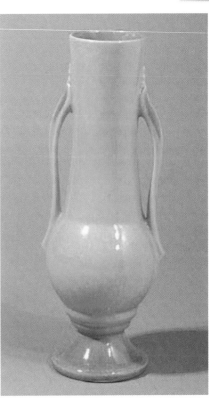

Orian footed vase
with bulbous base and two handles, yellow exterior
and blue-green interior, unmarked, 12 1/2″ by 4″.
$275-$325

Orian yellow ovoid planter
bruise to one handle and tiny nick under base, gold foil label, 4 3/4″ by 14 1/2″.

$250-$350

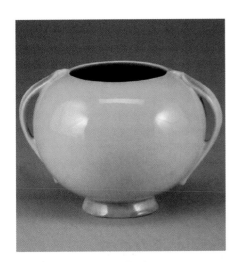

Orian yellow spherical vase
with buttressed handles, some grinding chips and
bruise to handle, unmarked, 6 1/4″ by 9″.
$175-$225

Orian squat vessal
with squat stepped base, in yellow and green,
unmarked, 7″ by 8″.
$200-$225

Orian yellow vase
with squat base and buttressed handles, unmarked,
9 1/4″ by 5 1/2″.

$250-$300

Panel

Part of the Rosecraft line from about 1920, Panel features realistic nudes and floral forms, mostly in one or two colors, on dark brown or green bodies. (This pattern should not be confused with Silhouette from three decades later, which also has nude and floral motifs but in a more stylized form.) Panel is marked with an "Rv" ink stamp.

Panel brown vase
with nudes in orange, used as a lamp base but not drilled (includes fittings), several chips to rim; pottery: 10″ tall.

$550-$650

Panel brown vase
with dandelions, "Rv" ink stamp, 7″ by 3 1/4″.

$275-$325

Panel brown flat vase
with nudes, two shallow scratches near base, "Rv" ink stamp, 8 1/2″ by 6″.

$550-$650

Panel green center bowl
with purple blossoms, "Rv" ink stamp, 9″ diameter.
$150-$200

Panel brown wall pocket
with Baneda pattern, "Rv" ink stamp, 9″ by 4 1/4″.
$200-$250

Panel brown wall pocket
with daisies, "Rv" ink stamp, 9" tall.

$250-$300

Panel flaring buttressed vase
with nudes, restoration to several lines from rim, "Rv" ink stamp, 11 1/2" tall.

$400-$500

Panel green wall pocket
with nude, short dark crazing line at seam of back and front (most likely in making), "Rv" ink stamp, 7" by 5".

$500-$600

Panel green vase
with nudes, repaired chips at rim and base, and some shallow scratches, "Rv" ink stamp, 10 1/4" by 5".

$375-$425

Pauleo

This Frederick Rhead design from about 1914 combines the names of Roseville co-founder George Young's daughter-in-law, Pauline, and his daughter, Leota. Commonly found as lamp bases, the simple forms were based on ancient vessels, and the glaze combinations are seemingly limitless. Pieces are frequently unmarked.

Pauleo decorated tall factory lamp base
with tulips on a gunmetal ground, in as-is condition (reglued cracks to rim, drilled hole to bottom, nick to body), raised circular mark 231, 16 1/2″ by 6 1/2″.

$275-$325

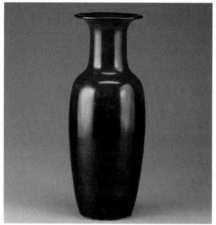

Pauleo classically shaped vase
covered in a fine variegated red glaze, several scratches to body and factory drill hole, unmarked, 20 3/4″ tall.

$1,100-$1,300

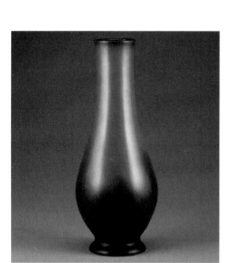

Pauleo bulbous vase
in smooth orange and brown glaze, a few minor abrasions to rim, unmarked, 18 1/4″ tall.

$650-$750

Pauleo factory lamp base
in a pink crackled glaze (rare), unmarked, 19″ tall.

$1,300-$1,500

Pauleo disk vase or bowl
in mottled green and pink glazes on a textured background, marked on the bottom with a "Pauleo Pottery" wafer, 7 1/2″ by 3″.

$1,000-$1,200

Pauleo baluster vase
with bulbous body, extremely tapered neck and flaring mouth, in a mottled red and ashen glaze, marked on the bottom with a "Pauleo Pottery" wafer, 10 1/2″ tall.

$1,000-$1,200

Peony

This line from 1942 features large irregular flower clusters on textured backgrounds that included salmon and green, green and tan, or gold and brown-green, rarely rusty brown. Pieces feature a raised mark, "Roseville U.S.A.," and a style number.

Peony green hanging basket
with crisp mold, nick to one petal, marked "U.S.A.," 5" by 7".

$110-$140

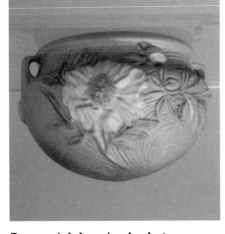

Peony pink hanging basket
several small chips to decoration, marked "U.S.A.," 5 1/2" by 7".

$175-$200

Three Peony pieces
pair of green double candlesticks (1153) with some chips to one, and pink cornucopia-shaped vase (170-6"), raised marks.

$90-$110/set

Peony green three-piece tea set
teapot (3), creamer (3-C), and sugar dish (3-S), small chip to base of sugar dish, and minor glaze bubbles to spout of teapot, raised marks.

$225-$275

Peony yellow ovoid vase
(661-3"), raised mark, 4 5/8" by 3 1/8".

$80-$100

Peony yellow tea set
(3), raised marks; teapot: 9" by 10 1/4".

$350-$400/set

Two Peony pieces
small pink planter (427-4") and yellow ovoid vase (67-12") with bruise and two restored chips, raised marks.

$125-$175/pair

Four Peony pieces

pair of yellow candlesticks (1151-2″), pink bowl (430-10″), and yellow vase (57-4″), all marked.

$150-$200/set

Two Peony pieces

yellow bulbous vase (63-8″) with several chips to flowers and leaves and pink conch shell-shaped piece (436) with fleck to edge of rim and very small bruise to one foot, raised marks.

$125-$175/pair

Peony green floor vase

(70-18″), minute fleck to one handle and small misfire to one leaf, raised mark.

$350-$400

Peony green flaring vase

(69-15″) with strong mold, small chip at rim, raised mark.

$275-$325

Peony pink pedestal

flat chip to rim, several nicks overall, marked "U.S.A."

$90-$110

Persian

With a strong art nouveau influence, Persian pieces (1908) often feature tight symmetrical designs of stylized scrolls and geometric shapes, with some naturalistic floral motifs, set off by narrow black borders. The line appears to have been limited to jardinières, pedestals, and planters. Pieces are unmarked.

Persian jardinière
(462), 5″ tall,

$250-$300;

and hanging basket, 3 3/4″ tall.

$400-$450

Persian hanging basket
small chip to one hole and two groups of spider lines to body, unmarked, 7 1/2″ tall.

$250-$300

Persian hanging basket
some fading of outlines, opposing 1″ hairlines and a bruise to rim, unmarked, 8 1/2″ tall.

$200-$225

Persian hanging basket
with bright coloration, spider lines to base and small chip to one handle, unmarked, 10″ tall.

$350-$400

Persian planter
with stylized pattern in pastel tones, chips to two feet, flecks to rim, unmarked, 4 1/4″ by 6 1/2″.

$150-$200

Pine Cone

The story of the Pine Cone design is a serendipitous tale of rejection and, ultimately, triumph. The pattern was designed by Frank Ferrel in the early 1900s, but variations were rejected by both Weller and Peters & Reed potteries as unworkable. A sample was also rejected by Roseville, and it languished for years until a Roseville salesman, Charles Snyder, became convinced of its marketability in 1931. The rest is history, and by some estimates, more than 150 styles were created. On backgrounds of blue, orange-brown-tan, or green, it features small ovoid cones with long pine needles on irregular-shaped branches, which may also form the handles of a given piece. In exceedingly rare instances, a pink background may be found. Sometimes unmarked, pieces bear marks that are both raised and impressed, and foil labels are also found. (A late-1940s version with a glossy finish is known as Pine Cone II or Modern.)

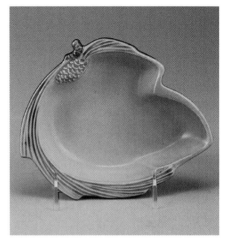

Pine Cone blue leaf-shaped dish or ashtray
(497), raised mark, 1 1/2″ by 4″.

$200-$250

Pine Cone blue basket
wave-shaped (408-6″) with small chip and nick to base ring, raised mark.

$175-$225

Pine Cone blue basket
(338-10″), some peppering to needles, impressed mark.

$400-$500

Pine Cone blue basket
(410-10″), raised mark.

$400-$500

Pine Cone blue hanging basket
minor scratches to tip, unmarked, 5 1/2″ by 8″.

$350-$400

Pine Cone blue bookends
in the shape of an open book, unmarked, 4 5/8″ by 5 1/4″ by 5 1/4″.

$375-$425/pair

Pine Cone blue bowl
(279-9″), impressed mark.

$250-$300

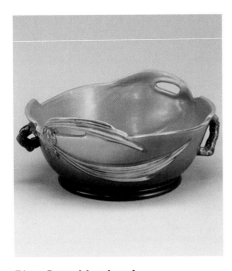

Pine Cone blue bowl
(321-9″), impressed mark.

$300-$350

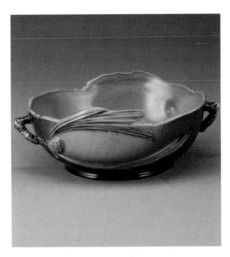

Pine Cone blue bowl
(355-8″), bruise to one handle and several small chips at base, impressed mark.

$175-$225

Pine Cone blue bowl
minute bruise to body, two shallow scratches near base, "flea bite" to one handle, unmarked, 4 1/4″ by 11 1/2″.

$250-$300

Pine Cone blue center bowl
hairline crack from rim and a few scratches, unmarked, 6″ by 16″.

$275-$325

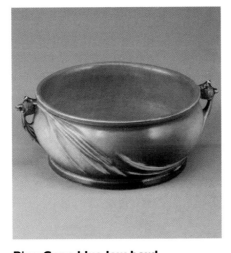

Pine Cone blue low bowl
(261-6″) with two small branch handles, nick to each handle.

$125-$175

Pine Cone blue ovoid bowl
(429-10″), raised mark.

$325-$375

Pine Cone blue candlesticks
(1099-4 1/2″), restoration and nick to rim of one, both marked.
$125-$175/pair

Pair of Pine Cone blue cups
(960-4″), raised marks.

$500-$600/pair

Pine Cone blue double dish
with strong mold, 6 1/2″ by 13″.

$600-$700

Pine Cone blue ewer
(851-15″), restoration to hairline on one handle, glaze inconsistency on one side, impressed mark.

$700-$800

Pine Cone blue ewer
(909-10″), impressed mark, and remnant of gold foil label.

$550-$650

Pine Cone blue dish rectangular
(430-12″), repaired chip at base, raised mark.

$150-$200

Pine Cone blue jardinière and pedestal
crisp mold, minor chips and spider lines to base of jardinière, hairline to one handle, pedestal has scaling to pine needle and handle (one touched up), and two repaired chips to rim, both unmarked; jardinière: 12″ by 15″.

$3,000-$4,000

Pine Cone blue jardinière
(403-10″) and pedestal, restoration to chip at base of jardinière, glaze chip to handle, clay burst to base of pedestal, some scratches to both, overall good condition.

$2,000-$2,500

Pine Cone blue dish wave-shaped
(427-8″), with repair to tip, raised mark.

$175-$225

Pine Cone blue planter
(124) with abrasion to rim, impressed mark, 5″ tall.

$225-$275

Pine Cone blue ovoid planter
soft mold, hairline around base of one handle, 4 3/4″ by 11 1/4″.

$225-$275

Pine Cone blue rectangular planter
(380-10″), several small chips to rim and decoration, impressed mark.
$750-$850

Pine Cone blue small planter
(456-6″) with 1/2″ line, raised marks.
$100-$150

Two Pine Cone blue smoking pieces
small leaf-shaped ashtray (499) and cigarette holder (498), raised marks; 4 3/4″ diameter and 2 3/4″ tall.
$450-$550/pair

Three Pine Cone blue tumblers
(414-5″), raised mark.
$800-$900/set

Pine Cone blue umbrella stand
(777-20″) with strong mold and color, raised mark.
$2,400-$2,600

Pine Cone blue urn
(912-15″), restoration to rim chip, impressed mark.
$1,700-$1,900

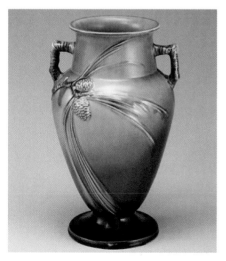

Pine Cone blue urn
restoration to base, unmarked, 14 1/4″ by 8 1/2″.
$600-$700

Pine Cone blue pitcher
(1321), good mold, impressed mark, 7 1/2″ tall.
$700-$800

Pine Cone blue canoe-shaped planter
(431-15″), minute grinding fleck to base, raised mark.
$425-$475

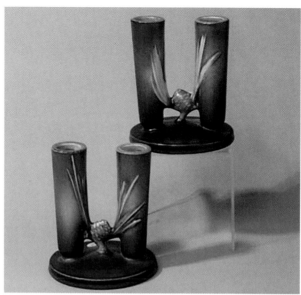

Pair of Pine Cone blue double bud vases
(1124), crack to center of one, both have a restored rim chip, impressed marks, 4 3/4″ by 4 1/4″.

$375-$425/pair

Pine Cone blue bud vase
foil label, 7 1/2″ by 4″.

$325-$375

Pine Cone blue bulbous vase
(689-6″), impressed mark.

$200-$250

Pine Cone blue bulbous vase
(709-10″), some peppering to rim, impressed mark.

$375-$425

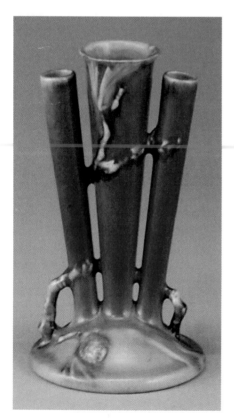

Pine Cone blue triple bud vase
unmarked, 8 1/2″.

$400-$500

Pine Cone blue bulbous vase
(849-10″) with buttressed base, reglued handle and peppering to rim, impressed mark.

$275-$325

Pine Cone blue cornucopia vase
very minor glaze miss at rim, faint impressed mark, 6″ by 6 1/2″.

$175-$225

Pine Cone blue cornucopia vase
(128-8″), deep crazing lines to tip, restoration to
two chips at base, impressed mark.
$110-$140

Pine Cone blue corseted vase
with squat base (712-12″), restoration to small chip
at rim, impressed mark.
$400-$450

Pine Cone blue corseted vase
with squat base (712-12″), very strong mold and
color, raised mark.
$700-$800

Pine Cone blue vase
corseted (814-7″), impressed mark.
$450-$500

Pine Cone blue flaring vase
with basket handle (936-10″), marked.
$400-$450

Pine Cone blue flaring pillow vase
(492-12″), strong mold and color, raised mark.
$1,400-$1,600

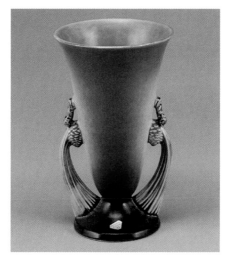

Pine Cone blue vase
flaring, foil label on body, 11 1/2″ by 6″.
$600-$700

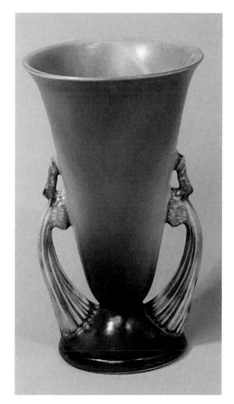

Pine Cone blue flaring vase
with two buttressed handles (747-10″), soft mold,
impressed mark.
$400-$500

Pine Cone blue vase
with squat base, obscured impressed mark, 8 1/4″
by 6 3/4″.

$400-$500

Pine Cone blue vase
(847-9″), small nick to rim, impressed mark.

$375-$425

Pine Cone blue flaring vase
(838-6″), small flake to rim, impressed mark.

$250-$300

**Pine Cone blue
fan vase**
(472-6″), overall
peppering, raised
mark.

$375-$425

Pine Cone blue pillow vase
(121-7″), impressed mark.

$275-$325

Pine Cone blue spherical vase
(746-7″), several small chips to base, some scratches, impressed mark.

$275-$325

Pine Cone blue squat vessel
(278-4″) with strong mold, impressed mark.

$300-$350

Pine Cone blue vase
(711-10″) with good mold and color, restoration to one handle, impressed mark.

$450-$550

Pine Cone blue triple wall pocket
(466), raised mark, 4 1/2″ by 9″.

$1,200-$1,500

Pine Cone brown ashtray
unmarked, 5″ wide.

$225-$275

Pine Cone brown basket
(339), restoration to chip at base, impressed mark, 11″ by 13 1/4″ by 9 3/4″.

$550-$650

Pine Cone brown hanging basket
unmarked, 5 1/2″ tall.

$250-$300

Pine Cone brown hanging basket
short and shallow horizontal line to rim, and a few minute flecks to body and hanging holes, marked "U.S.A.," 5 1/2″ tall.

$125-$175

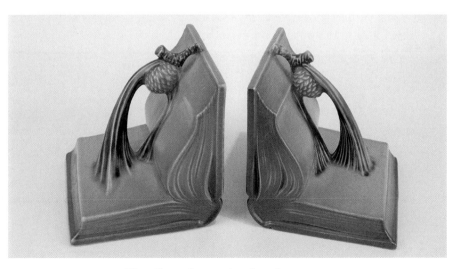

Pine Cone brown bookends
impressed mark, minor flaking, 5 3/8″ by 5″ by 5″.

$450-$500/pair

Pine Cone brown center bowl
(322-12˝), impressed mark.

$225-$275

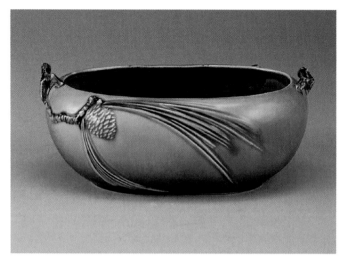

Pine Cone brown ovoid bowl
unmarked, 4˝ by 11˝.

$175-$225

Four Pine Cone brown candlesticks
two triple (1106-5 1/2˝) and two single (1123), hairlines to two, raised marks.

$550-$650/set

Pine Cone brown cider set
with pitcher (415-9˝) and four tumblers (414-5˝), raised marks.

$1,400-$1,500/set

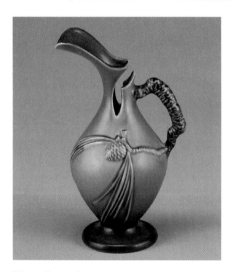

Pine Cone brown ewer
(909-10˝), raised mark.

$375-$425

Pine Cone brown flowerpot
(633-5˝) and under plate, minute flecks to foot ring, raised mark.

$275-$325

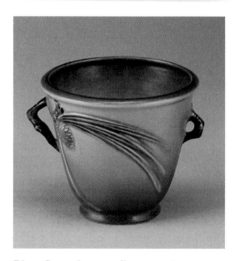

Pine Cone brown flowerpot
(633-5˝), missing under plate, very tight short line to interior rim, raised mark, 5 1/4˝ by 6 1/2˝.

$110-$140

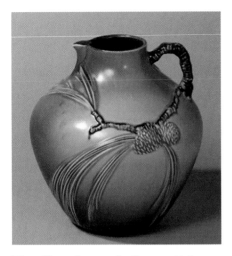

Pine Cone brown bulbous pitcher
several minor nicks to pine cones, unmarked, 9 1/2˝ by 8 1/2˝.

$450-$550

Pine Cone brown water pitcher with ice lip
(1321), clay pimple to one pine cone, a couple of small pock marks, and restoration around base, impressed mark.

$325-$375

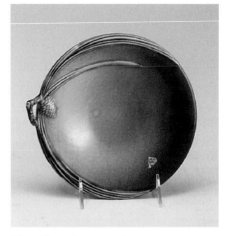

Pine Cone brown plate
several long cracks (possibly reglued for stabilization) and a small chip to edge, remnant of foil label to front of plate, 8 1/4˝ wide.

$150-$200

Five brown Pine Cone pieces
mint spherical pitcher (1321) with ice lip, and four cups (960-4), three of which are in as-is condition (chips, crack), impressed mark; pitcher: 8˝ by 8 3/4˝.

$550-$650/set

Three Pine Cone brown pieces
tall footed vase, vase with squat base (842-8˝), and small jardinière (632-3˝), impressed marks on two; tall vase: 9 3/4˝.

$750-$850/set

Two Pine Cone brown pieces
in as-is condition (chips, repairs, etc.): cornucopia vase (126-6˝) and an ashtray (499), raised marks.

$90-$110/pair

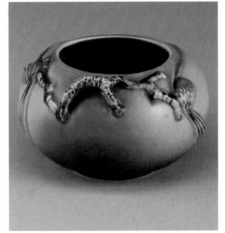

Pine Cone brown spherical jardinière
(278-4˝), impressed mark.

$225-$275

Pine Cone brown jardinière and pedestal
with strong mold, extensive restoration to both jardinière and pedestal, unmarked; jardinière: 11˝ tall, pedestal: 18˝ tall.

$600-$700

Two Pine Cone brown pieces
jardinière (632-4˝) and low bowl (354-6˝) with line from rim and reglued handle, both marked.
$150-$200/pair

Pine Cone brown spherical jardinière
(632-7˝), impressed mark.
$400-$450

Pair of Pine Cone brown bookend planters
(459), minor firing chip to bottom ring of one, raised mark, 5 1/4˝ by 5˝ by 5˝.
$800-$1,000/pair

Pine Cone brown planter
(124), nicks to branch and base, impressed mark, 5˝ by 5 1/4˝.
$175-$225

Pine Cone brown rectangular planter
(468-8˝), two flecks to rim, raised mark.
$225-$275

Pine Cone brown urn
(848-10˝) with very crisp mold, raised mark.
$450-$550

Pine Cone brown urn
(844-8˝) with crisp mold, glaze flake inside both handles (possibly in manufacture), raised mark.
$350-$400

Pine Cone brown footed urn
(713-14˝), strong mold and color, restoration to rim and base chip, impressed mark.
$550-$650

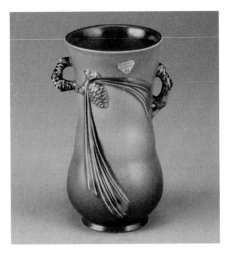

Pine Cone brown bulbous vase
(841-7″) with very strong mold, foil label to body,
impressed mark.

$250-$300

Pine Cone brown triple bud vase
unmarked, 8 1/2″ by 4 1/2″.

$350-$400

Pine Cone brown corseted vase
(712-12″), impressed mark.

$500-$600

Pine Cone brown bud vase
(112-7″), impressed mark.

$300-$350

Pine Cone brown flaring vase
(747-10″), very minor restoration to one "handle"
near base, impressed mark.

$225-$275

Pine Cone brown floor vase
(913-18″) with good mold and color, repair to rim
and base, incised mark.

$700-$900

**Pine Cone brown four-sided pillow
vase**
(114-8″), soft mold, small nick to one pine cone,
impressed mark.

$350-$450

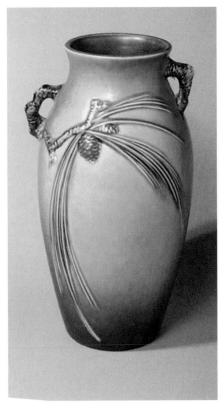

Pine Cone brown ovoid vase
(806-12″), impressed mark.

$600-$700

Pine Cone brown pillow vase
(845-8˝), foil label on body.

$275-$325

Pine Cone brown vase
(907-7˝) with flaring rim and good mold, fleck at
base, impressed mark.

$275-$325

Pine Cone brown vase
unmarked, 7˝ by 6˝.

$175-$225

Two Pine Cone brown pieces
small wave-shaped basket (408-6˝) and cornucopia-shaped vase (126-6˝), both marked.

$450-$550/pair

Pine Cone brown spherical vessel
(745-7˝), flat chip to base ring (shows slightly on
side), impressed mark.

$250-$300

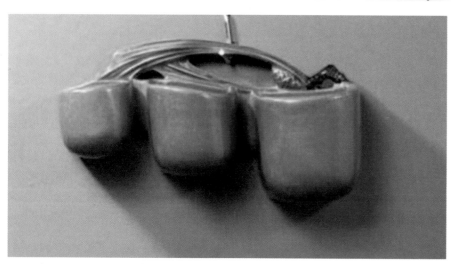

Pine Cone brown triple wall pocket
(466), minor burst bubble to edge, raised mark, 4 1/2˝ by 9˝.

$450-$550

Pine Cone brown wall shelf
touch-up to tip of branch, minute fleck to rim,
raised mark, 8 3/4˝ tall.

$125-$175

Two Pine Cone vases
one brown (extensive restoration), one green (restoration to rim), foil labels on both, 8 1/2″ and 10 1/2″ tall.

$225-$275/pair

Five Pine Cone green pieces
pair of triple candlesticks (1106-5 1/2″) with chips to base of one, chip, fleck, and line to the other; single candlestick (451-4″) with repair to base; a bud vase (479-7″) with several chips; and planter, all marked.

$350-$400/set

Pine Cone green basket
(408-6″), raised mark, 5 1/2″ by 6 1/2″ by 3 5/8″.
$400-$450

Pine Cone green ewer
(851-15″), impressed mark.
$700-$800

Pine Cone green ewer
(416-18″), restored chip to spout, and minor firing flaw to base, raised mark.
$400-$450

Pine Cone green handled bowl
(410-10″), several repairs to cracks on handle, raised mark.

$125-$175

Pine Cone green center bowl
short tight line from rim and minor grinding chips, unmarked, 4 1/4″ by 11″.

$110-$140

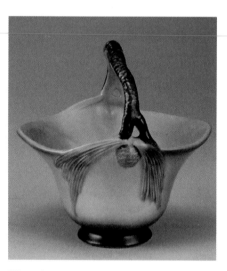

Pine Cone green basket
(409-8″), raised mark.

$300-$350

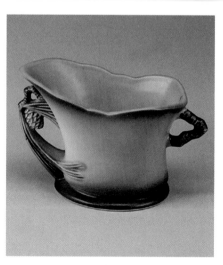

Two Pine Cone green pieces
rectangular dish (430-12″) with strong mold and gravy boat (455-6″) with chip to handle, raised marks.

$225-$275/pair

Pine Cone green jardinière
(632-5″), nick to one pine cone, foil label to body and impressed mark.

$110-$140

Pine Cone green jardinière
(632-8″) with strong mold, chips to base and line from rim, foil label.

$325-$375

Pine Cone green pitcher
(457-7″) with strong mold, raised mark.

$175-$225

Pine Cone green footed planter
with scalloped rim (458F-5″), glaze scaling to handles, impressed mark.

$150-$200

Pine Cone green canoe-shaped planter
(431-15″), 1/2″ flat chip to base ring, raised mark.
$125-$175

Pine Cone green bulbous vase
(856-12″), impressed mark.
$450-$550

Pine Cone green vessel
unmarked, 5 1/8″ by 4 7/8″ by 4 1/2″.
$175-$225

Pine Cone green flaring vase
(492-12″), restoration to rim and dividing bar, marked.
$300-$350

Pine Cone green flaring vase
(747-10″) with three small flecks and chip to base ring, impressed mark.
$200-$250

Pine Cone green pillow vase
(845-8″), foil label to body and impressed mark.
$275-$325

Pine Cone green spherical vessel
(261-6″), repaired chip at rim and restored chip at base, impressed mark.
$90-$110

Pine Cone green spherical footed vessel
grinding chips to corners of foot, and reglued handle, unmarked, 7 1/2″ by 7″
$100-$150

Pine Cone green squat vessel
with strong mold, unmarked, 6 3/4″ by 4 1/4″.
$300-$350

Two Pine Cone green pieces
pillow vase (121-7″) and low bowl (354-6″), impressed marks.

$275-$325/pair

Two Pine Cone green pieces
small boat-shaped vessel (455-6″) and double vase (473-8″), raised marks.

$350-$400/pair

Two Pine Cone green pieces
rare cylindrical vase with flaring rim (short tight line to one leaf), and triple
bud vase, unmarked, 8 1/4″ tall each.

$300-$350/pair

Two Pine Cone green vases
(one is 839-6″), small chip to one pine cone on larger, one marked; second vase
9 1/4″ by 4 3/4″.

$325-$375/pair

Pine Cone Modern planter or window box
(468-8″), raised mark.

$400-$500

Pine Cone Modern planter
(472-8″), raised mark.

$400-$500

Two Pine Cone Modern pieces
basket (408-6″), raised mark,

$350-$450;

and candleholder (451-4″), raised mark.

$350-$400

Pine Cone Modern double serving tray
(462), unmarked, 6″ by 13 1/4″.

$350-$450

Poppy

Introduced in 1938, Poppy features flowers, both in full bloom and in buds, on slender waving stems. Backgrounds may be yellow-brown, pale yellow and dusty blue, green and orange-pink, salmon and yellow, or pink, yellow, and brown. Marks are often impressed, rarely raised, and sometimes pieces are unmarked.

Poppy brown vessel on squat base
(873-9″), restoration around base, impressed mark, rare.

$450-$550

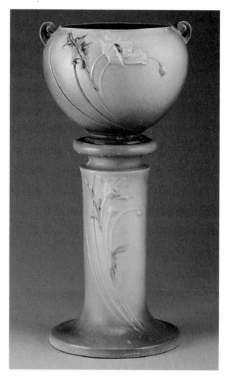

Poppy green jardinière and pedestal set
1/4″ chip and clay pimple to base of jardinière, unmarked; jardinière: 10″ tall, pedestal: 16″ tall.

$700-$800

Poppy gray-blue planter and double candleholder
(341-7″), impressed mark, 8″ by 8 1/2″.

$225-$275

Poppy green console set
consisting of a large four-sided center bowl and a pair of candlesticks (1129), 1/2″ chip to foot ring and two minor flecks to rim of bowl, impressed marks on candlesticks; bowl: 5 1/2″ by 16″.

$175-$225

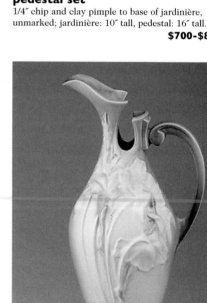

Poppy green ewer
(880-18″), minor bruise to one petal, impressed mark.

$500-$600

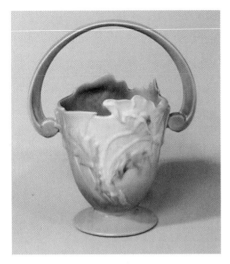

Poppy green basket
(347-10˝), raised mark.

$250-$300

Poppy green bulbous vase
(875-10˝) with repair and bruise to base, and nick to flower, impressed mark.

$150-$200

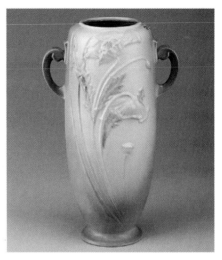

Poppy green ovoid floor vase
(829-18˝), impressed mark.

$600-$700

Two Poppy green pieces
flaring vessel (866-6˝) and vase, both marked (one obscured); vase: 7˝ tall.

$225-$275/pair

Poppy pink ewer
(876-10˝), good mold, impressed mark.

$250-$300

Poppy pink ewer
(880-18˝), good mold, minor peppering to spout, impressed mark.

$550-$650

Poppy squat vessel
with handles, unmarked, 4˝ by 7 5/8˝ by 5 7/8˝.

$250-$350

Two Poppy pink vessels
small jardinière (642-3˝) and low bowl (336-5˝), short tight line to rim of jardinière, impressed marks, silver foil label on one.

$110-$140/pair

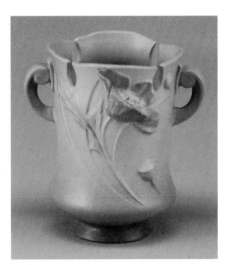

Poppy pink vase
(869-7˝), short firing line to base, impressed mark.

$125-$175

Primrose

From 1936, Primrose features tiny white blossoms on spindly stems emerging from a cluster of green leaves. Backgrounds are blue, brown-yellow-tan, or salmon pink. Pieces have impressed marks.

Primrose blue bulbous jardinière
(634-7˝), nick with several lines to one handle, impressed mark.

$90-$110

Primrose blue jardinière
(634-8˝) and pedestal, jardinière has 6˝ line to body (goes through to interior) and several quarter-size patches of glaze scaling; pedestal has restoration to crack around base, impressed mark.

$375-$425

Two Primrose blue pieces
vase (761-6˝) with peppering to one side and spherical jardinière (284-4˝), impressed marks, one also has foil label.

$225-$275/pair

Two Primrose brown pieces
squat jardinière with soft mold (284-4˝) and vase (763-7˝) with restoration to 1/2˝ rim chip, impressed marks.

$200-$250/pair

Primrose blue vase
(772-14˝), two minor flakes to base, impressed mark.

$400-$450

Primrose blue vase
made into a lamp base, crack from base, pottery
height: 8 1/2″.

$80-$100

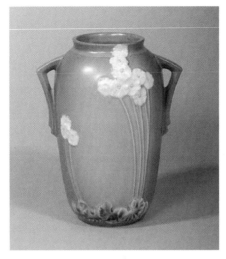

Primrose blue ovoid vase
(770-10″), impressed mark.

$300-$350

Primrose brown bulbous jardinière
(634-5″), impressed mark.

$250-$300

Primrose pink urn
(764-7″), marked.

$70-$90

Primrose pink spherical jardinière
(285-6 1/2″), impressed mark.

$125-$150

Primrose pink wall pocket
(1277-8″), impressed mark.

$550-$600

Two Primrose brown vases
one bulbous (767-8″) with touch-up to corner
of one handle and to small rim chip, and one
shouldered (760-6″), impressed marks.

$175-$225/pair

Three Primrose pink candlesticks
one triple (1113) and a pair (1105-4 1/2″),
impressed marks; triple: 5 1/2″ by 5 1/2″

$275-$325/set

Two Primrose pink pieces
vase (762-7″) and cornucopia (125) with small rim
chip, impressed marks; cornucopia: 6 1/2″ by 5″.

$175-$200/pair

Quaker

From the first quarter of the 20th century, these creamware pieces have a band of jolly Quakers smoking pipes around the tops of the vessels. All are unmarked.

Quaker cup or jar
(may have had lid), unmarked, cracks,
4 3/8″ by 3 1/2″.

$90-$120

Raymor

Almost the last gasp for Roseville, Raymor—designed by Ben Siebel and introduced in 1953—did not meet with the success that the company had hoped for. This line of sleek, elliptical forms with a high gloss includes Modern Artware and Modern Stoneware, and a Gourmet group from 1954. Pieces feature raised or impressed marks. Now being embraced by collectors of modernist designs, this pattern still represents a good value for beginners.

Raymor/Modern Artware lantern wall pocket
covered in a glossy chartreuse glaze, three small chips to one edge, impressed 711, and paper labels, 10″ tall.

$300-$350

Two Raymor bowls
a brown "Lug Fruit," (192), and a covered baking dish in ivory, indistinct style number.
$50-$60/pair

Rosecraft Color

From 1916, the Color line of Rosecraft has more than 60 shapes in solid colors of blue, green, red, and yellow. Pieces are often unmarked or have an "Rv″ stamp.

Rosecraft Color pink hanging basket
with three loop handles, unmarked, 4″ by 7″.

$75-$100

Rosecraft Vintage

The Rosecraft Vintage line from 1924 was also strongly influenced by art nouveau design, with stylized grapevines ringing classically shaped vessels of dark brown. Pieces often feature an "Rv" ink stamp.

Rosecraft Vintage jardinière
two nicks to base, 7" by 9".

$200-$250

Rosecraft Vintage jardiniére
with very strong mold, no visible mark, 9 1/4" by 12".

$375-$425

Rosecraft Vintage bowl
with crisp mold, "Rv" ink stamp, 2" by 7 1/2".

$225-$275

Two Rosecraft Vintage jardinières;
1/4" chip and two bruises to base of one, some minor flecks to both, "Rv" ink stamps, 6 1/4" and 5 1/4" tall.

$350-$400/pair

Rosecraft Vintage rectangular planter
complete with liner, "Rv" ink stamp, 5 1/2" by 11".

$800-$900

Rosecraft Vintage barrel-shaped vase
a few shallow scratches, "Rv" ink stamp, 6 1/2" by 3 1/2".

$175-$225

Rosecraft Vintage double bud vase
nick to base, "Rv" ink stamp, 5" by 7 1/2".

$400-$450

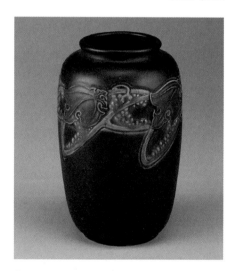

Rosecraft Vintage bulbous vase
drilled hole to base, "Rv" ink stamp, 8" by 4 1/2".

$200-$250

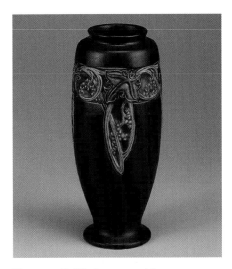

Rosecraft Vintage ovoid vase
"Rv" ink stamp, 12 1/4" by 4 1/4".
$800-$900

Rosecraft Vintage bulbous vase
with two buttressed handles, bruise to one berry,
"Rv" ink stamp, 4" by 3 1/4".
$175-$225

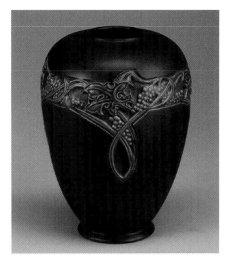

Rosecraft Vintage bulbous vase
"Rv" ink stamp, 10 1/2" by 7".
$550-$650

Two Rosecraft Vintage pieces
ovoid vase and a small bowl, "Rv" ink stamps; vase:
5" tall.
$275-$325/pair

Rosecraft Vintage wall pocket
"Rv" ink stamp, 9" tall.
$375-$425

**Rosecraft Vintage classically
shaped vase**
with strong mold, "Rv" ink stamp, 8 1/2" by 6".
$500-$550

Two Rosecraft Vintage vases
barrel-shaped vase (painted over glaze
flaking) and bulbous (kiln "kiss" to
body), "Rv" ink stamp, each 6 1/4" tall.
$325-$375/pair

Rosecraft Vintage wall pocket
small chip to tip, "Rv" ink stamp, 8 1/2" tall.
$225-$275

Rosecraft Vintage squat vessel
"Rv" ink stamp, 3" by 4 1/2".
$200-$250

Royal Capri

Another line that failed to meet expectations, Royal Capri, with its mottled glossy and matt gold finish, was produced near the end of Roseville Pottery's existence. Pieces are hard to find in mint condition. They feature raised marks.

Royal Capri scalloped bowl
(526-7″), minor wear to gold at rim, raised mark.
$175-$200

Four pieces of Royal Capri
vase (579-8″) is 8 1/2″ tall,

$225-$275;

scalloped bowl (527-7″) on right is 7 1/2 in diameter,

$200-$225;

console bowl (526-7″) center is 7 1/2″ diameter,

$200-$225;

and small footed pot (faint mark) foreground is 2 3/4″ tall.

$200-$225

Rozane Line, 1917

Often identified as Rozane Line or Rozane 1917, these wares are at the opposite end of the design spectrum from Rozane Royal. It has heavy floral and leaf patterns on a textured body, usually cream or pale green. Pieces are usually unmarked and rarely stamped.

Rozane 1917 green compote and flower frog
base chips to both, neither marked; compote: 6″ by 9″; frog: 2 1/2″ by 1 1/8″.

$250-$300/pair

Rozane 1917 jardinière
unmarked, 8 1/2″ by 9″.

$125-$175

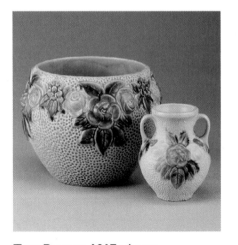

Two Rozane 1917 pieces
green jardinière (bruise to rim and repairs to flowers) and ivory vase, Rozane stamp mark to one; jardinière: 9″ tall.

$150-$200/pair

Two Rozane 1917 pieces
center bowl and handled vase; line to rim and some small chips to decoration on bowl; repaired handles to vase, one marked; bowl: 7 1/2″ diameter; vase: 5 1/4″ tall.

$110-$140/pair

Rozane Pattern

This line from 1941 bears the Rozane name, but the similarities to earlier Rozane lines end there. These shapes are mostly sleek and modern, with bright solid colors of blue, green, and terra cotta, and a few in mottled matte glazes that blend pastel shades. Pieces have raised marks.

Rozane Pattern footed vase with flaring rim
(11-15″), covered in a mottled blue-green matte glaze, raised mark.

$450-$500

Two Rozane Pattern pieces
vase (7-9″) and urn (5-8″) with minor bruise to rim, both covered in a mottled blue-green matte glaze, raised marks.

$300-$350/pair

Two Rozane Pattern vases
with buttressed base, (9-10″) with several chips to inner foot ring, and (10-12″), both covered in a glossy vermillion glaze, raised marks.

$250-$275/pair

Six Rozane Pattern pieces
1940s, four in glossy blue: low bowl (396-10″), vase (2-6″), large footed cornucopia (2), and feather ornament (2) with broken tip; and two in glossy terra cotta: two-handled vase (1-6″) and fish ornament (1), raised marks; cornucopia: 5″ by 12″.

$350-$400/set

Two Rozane Pattern spherical vessels
(398-6″) in mottled matte glazes, one blue and one green, raised marks.

$400-$450/pair

Rozane/ Rozane Royal

Designed to compete with similar lines by Weller and Rookwood, Rozane (which combined the names Roseville and Zanesville) was introduced shortly after the turn of the 19th century, and the artists who created these pieces were left to their own stylistic devices. Many pieces have floral motifs, others featured portraits, some hunting dogs, still others had harvest themes or birds. Though most backgrounds are a glossy black-brown, others are called Royal Light and have ivory or pastel tones. Pieces are often artist signed or stamped "Rozane RPCo." or "Rozane Royal Ware" on a wafer/seal.

Two Rozane ewers
both with floral decoration, right, signed W. Meyers, 10 7/8″ tall,

left, with Rozane wafer, 9 1/2″ tall.

$350-$450

$250-$350

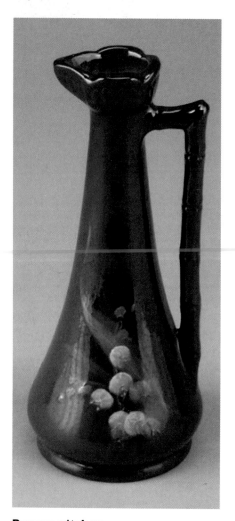

Rozane pitcher
painted with Lily of the Valley, nick and repaired chips to base, Rozane Ware seal, 7 1/2″ tall.
$110-$140

Rozane Royal Dark pitcher
painted with cherries, illegible artist's initials, marked "ROZANE 890 RPCO," 12 1/4″ by 6 1/2″.
$600-$700

Rozane Royal Dark pitcher
painted by W. Meyers with branches of cherries, lifting of overglaze (some touch-up), Rozane wafer, 15 3/4″ tall.
$200-$250

Rozane Royal Dark bottle-shaped vase
painted with brown carnations, stamped "ROZANE/ RPCO/919," 8″ by 4 1/2″.

$175-$225

Rozane jardinière and pedestal
painted by W. Myers with yellow tea roses, flakes and scratches to both pieces, chips to foot of pedestal, artist-signed on pedestal, 32″ tall overall.

$900-$1,100

Rozane Royal Dark tall vase
painted with yellow and brown daisies, a few minor flecks to body and rim, stamped "ROZANE 837 RPCO."; 13″ by 7″.

$225-$275

Rozane bulbous vase
1/4″ filled-in chip to base and several flecks, stamped mark, 4″ tall.

$90-$110

Rozane Royal Dark bud vase
painted with palm fronds on a black to green ground, small bruises to rim, stamped "Rozane RPCO/ W.H.," 8″ tall.

$125-$175

Rozane Royal Dark bulbous vase
painted with poppies (?), stamped "ROZANE 806 RPCO."; 8″ by 4 1/2″.

$750-$850

Rozane teapot
with floral decoration, impressed mark, "935 RPCo.," 7 1/4" tall with lid.

$450-$550

Rozane Royal Dark vase
with whiplash handles, probably painted by Dunlavy, with branches of blackberries (very rare), restoration to drill hole on bottom and to handle, a few scratches, marked "D" on body, 15 3/4" by 6 1/2".

$175-$225

Rozane Royal Dark bulbous cabinet vase
painted with branch of green leaves by ER or FR, minute nick to rim, stamped "Rozane/RPCo/(artist signature)," 4" by 3 1/2".

$80-$100

Rozane Royal Dark ovoid vase
painted with a yellow crocus, pockmarks and scratches, impressed mark, 6 1/2" by 3 3/4".

$150-$200

Rozane Royal Dark tear-shaped vase
painted by H. Dunlavy with a Turkish man in profile, hairline from rim, Rozane wafer and artist's signature, 8" by 5".

$1,100-$1,300

Rozane Royal Dark pillow vase
shape No. 882, hand-painted with a hunting dog with a pheasant in its mouth, signed "Timberlake," marked with raised stamp, "Rozane Royal Ware," 10 3/4" by 9" by 6 1/4".

$3,500-$4,500

Rozane Royal Light vase
painted by Mae Timberlake with yellow daffodils, small bruise to rim, signed "Mae Timberlake" with Rozane wafer, 10 3/4" tall.

$500-$600

Two Rozane Royal Dark two-handled vases
one painted with violets, both stamped, one artist signed "EC," 4 1/2" tall each.

$175-$225/pair

Rozane Royal Light vase
painted with flowers, Rozane Royal wafer, 10 1/2" tall.

$350-$450

Rozane Royal Light footed bowl
painted with flowers, unmarked, 5" tall.

$350-$400

Two Rozane vases
both with stamped wafers, left: Royal Light with lilies, 8 1/8" tall,

right, Royal Dark with pansies, 7 5/8" tall.

$250-$350

$200-$300

Rozane Royal Light vase
painted with roses, drilled base, old shop label, 14 1/2" tall.

$450-$550

Rozane Royal Light spherical jardinière
on three feet, painted with lavender, white, and gray tulips, fine overall crazing, touched-up nick to inner rim, a couple of pock marks, and glaze flakes to feet, unmarked, 10" by 13".

$110-$140

Russco

Introduced in 1934, the Russco shapes have a strong art deco influence, but the glazes are often freeform, either blended or crystalline, green and beige or tan and brown being the most common. Some have interiors with iridescent surfaces. Pieces are unmarked or have paper labels.

Russco urn
in amber and gold crystalline glazes, small grinding chips, unmarked, 8 1/4″ by 6″.

$90-$110

Russco bulbous vase
with flaring rim in amber and gold crystalline glazes, unmarked, 10″ by 6 1/2″.

$350-$450

Russco vase
in gold and green crystalline glazes, repair and nicks to 3″ section of base, unmarked, 6 1/2″ by 6 1/2″.

$250-$300

Russco faceted flaring bowl
exterior in gold crystalline, interior in green and brown, unmarked, 4″ by 8″.

$150-$175

Russco urn
in green and beige crystalline glazes, minute fleck to rim and restoration to small chip at base, unmarked, 8 1/4″ by 6″.

$70-$90

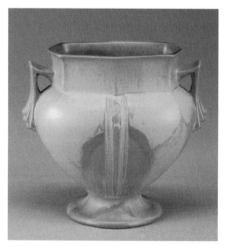

Russco orange-yellow footed vase
some tiny nicks to rim and base, unmarked, 7 1/2″ by 7 1/2″.

$125-$175

Two Russco pieces
flaring vase with restoration to one handle and base and double bud vase, both in green and beige crystalline glazes, unmarked, 8 1/4″ by 4″ and 8 1/2″ by 4″.

$200-$250/pair

Savona

The fluted, bulbous profile of Savona (mid-1920s) is accented by evenly spaced floral garlands on some pieces. Bright glossy solid colors include green and yellow, plus the subtler dusty blue, salmon, and ivory. Pieces are unmarked or have foil/paper labels.

Savona classically shaped vase
in blue-gray, unmarked, 12″ by 5 1/2″.
$200-$250

Pair of Savona urns
one apricot and one blue, peppering and restoration to a couple of areas at base, and opposing lines to rim of apricot urn, unmarked, 12″ by 7″ each.

$300-$400/pair

Savona blue console set
black paper label on bowl; candlesticks: 4″ by 4″; bowl: 4″ by 10″.

$275-$325/set

Savona yellow covered vessel
black paper label, 4″ by 8″.

$800-$900

Savona green four-sided vase
with touch-ups to two shallow chips on bottom ring (not visible on side), unmarked, 10 1/2″ by 3″.

$325-$350

Savona blue wall pocket
unmarked, 8 1/4″ tall.

$450-$550

Savona apricot bulbous vase
1/2″ bruise to one handle, unmarked, 6″ by 5 1/2″.

$150-$200

Savona green classically shaped vase
with burst bubbles around rim and base, unmarked, 12″ by 6 1/2″.

$250-$300

Savona ivory console set
hairline to one handle on each candlestick, 4″ line to bowl (does not go through), silver foil label on bowl; candlesticks: 4″ by 4″; bowl: 2 1/2″ by 10 1/2″.

$200-$225/set

Savona yellow classically shaped vase
unmarked, 12 1/4″ by 6″.

$250-$300

Silhouette

This line from 1950 is a mix of stylistic influences, sleek and chunky, bulbous and angular. With panels of female nudes or floral motifs on dark backgrounds, the bodies are muted solid colors, usually of blue-green, raspberry, brown, and white. Pieces feature raised marks or are stamped "U.S.A."

Silhouette blue basket
(710-10″) with panels of tropical blossoms, raised mark.

$70-$90

Four Silhouette pieces
red double planter (757-9″) with nick to base, two ovoid planters (779-5″) in red and white with oak leaves, and small white pitcher (716-6″) with acorns, all marked.

$225-$275/set

Silhouette brown hanging basket
embossed with ivy, stamped "U.S.A.," 4 1/4″ by 5 1/2″.

$150-$175

Silhouette brown box
(740) with branch and blossom, raised mark, 3″ by 4 1/2″.

$175-$225

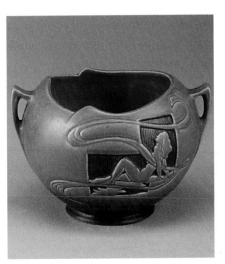

Silhouette brown bulbous vase
(742-6″) with 1″ bruise to base, raised mark.

$425-$475

Two Silhouette pieces
small brown ewer (716-6″) and white squat vessel
(741-4″); pitcher: 6 1/2″ tall.

$125-$175/pair

Silhouette pink vase
(783-7″) with female nude in profile, raised mark, 7 7/8″ by 7 3/8″ by 3 3/4″.

$650-$750

Silhouette covered box
with blooming branch (740), some flat chips to lid
and to base, raised mark, 2 3/4″ by 4 1/4″.

$35-$45

Silhouette pink wall pocket
(766-8″) with ivy leaves, raised mark.

$250-$300

**Three
Silhouette
pieces**
one green and one
white with branch
of leaves, and one
brown with oak
leaf (repair to
one corner), all
marked.

$125-$175/set

Snowberry

Gardeners may know the plant on this line of pottery as "symphoricarpos," while others will quickly recognize the clumps of white berries that give it its name. Introduced in 1947, this pattern also has a special letter code to identify shapes. Colors are a blend of variegated green and tan, pink-tan to burgundy, and blue to mauve. Most pieces have raised marks.

Snowberry blue basket
(1BK-7˝), raised mark, 7 7/8˝ by 7˝ by 3 3/8˝.

$175-$225

Snowberry blue hanging basket
unmarked, 5 1/4˝ by 8˝.

$150-$200

Snowberry blue candleholder
(1CS1), raised mark, 3 3/4˝ by 2˝.

$40-$60

Two Snowberry pieces
blue chalice vase (IUR-8˝) and pink ashtray (colored-in stilt pull chips), both marked; ashtray: 5 1/4˝ diameter.

$110-$140/pair

Pair of Snowberry blue cornucopia vases
(1CC-6˝), minor flat chip to base, fleck to rim of one (shows slightly on side), small fleck to base of the other, raised marks.

$100-$125/pair

Three Snowberry blue pieces
pair of ewers (ITK-6˝) and console bowl (IBL2-12) with small chips to rim and nick to handle, raised marks.

$250-$300/set

Snowberry blue three-piece tea set
nicks to spout of teapot, cracks to creamer (1C), all marked.

$225-$275/set

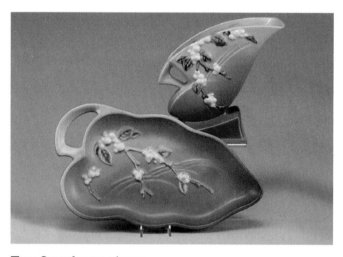

Two Snowberry pieces
blue leaf-shaped tray (1BL1-12) and pillow vessel (1FH-7˝) with small chip to rim, both marked.

$100-$150/pair

Three Snowberry green pieces
rectangular planter (IWX), round dish (IBLI-6˝) with small chip to rim and bruise to berry, and hanging basket with opposing cracks; two marked; hanging basket: 6˝ tall.

$225-$275/set

Two Snowberry pieces
green basket (IBK-10˝) and pink cornucopia vase (1CC-8˝), raised marks.
$275-$325

Snowberry green candlesticks
(1CS1), raised mark.

$225-$275

Snowberry green basket
(1BK-8″), raised mark.

$250-$300

Snowberry green jardinière
(IJ-8) and pedestal (IP-8), bruise to top of pedestal, both marked.

$550-$650

Two Snowberry pieces
green urn (IUR-8″) with short line to base (most likely in making) and pink wall pocket (IWP-8″), both marked.

$225-$275/pair

Three Snowberry pieces
pair of pink bud vases (IBV-7″) with small chips to base of one and green hanging basket (chip to one handle and line from rim), vases marked; basket: 8″ diameter.

$125-$175/set

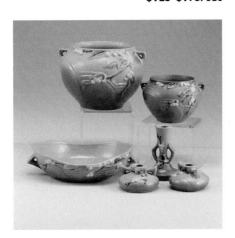

Six Snowberry pieces
pair of low pink candlesticks (ICS1), tall pink candlestick (ICS2) with small filled-in chip, pink bowl (IBL-8″) with chip to rim, green jardinière (IJ-4), and pink jardinière (IJ-6″), all marked.

$300-$350/set

Four Snowberry pieces
pink ewer (ITK10) with chips to base, small pink dish, pink vase (IVI-7″) with fleck to base and glaze chip to rim, and green vase (IV-6″), all marked.

$250-$300/set

Five Snowberry pieces
pink cornucopia vase with glaze scaling, possibly in making; two green bowls with chip to one; green vase; and blue leaf-shaped tray with small chip, all marked.

$225-$275/set

Snowberry pink tea set
(1) with clay burst to handle of creamer (in the firing), raised marks; teapot: 7 1/4″ by 10 1/2″.

$250-$300/set

Pair of Snowberry pink hanging baskets
some minor nicks and minor abrasion to one hanging hole, unmarked, 5″ tall each.

$175-$225/pair

Two Snowberry pieces
pink bud vase (IVI-7″) with large chips and blue bulbous vase (IV2-10″) with repairs to rim, raised marks.

$110-$140/pair

Snowberry pink cornucopia vase
(1CC-6″), raised mark, 6″ by 4″ by 5 1/4″.

$100-$140

Snowberry pink floor vase
(IV-18″), glazed over or touched-up nick to one handle, raised mark.

$375-$425

Snowberry pink footed vase
(1UR-8″), raised mark, 8 3/8″ by 6 1/2″ by 5 1/4″.

$100-$150

Sunflower

Introduced in 1930 and now one of the most popular Roseville lines, these pieces are ringed with large yellow blossoms on bending stems that march in lock step at regular intervals. In descending order on the rough textured surface are brown, green, and blue, mottled with ivory or yellow. Pieces are unmarked or with black paper labels.

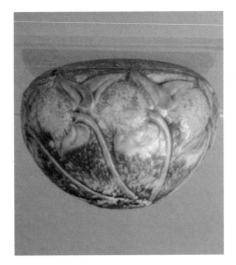

Sunflower hanging basket
1 1/2″ spider line from rim, unmarked, 5″ by 7″.
$450-$550

Pair of Sunflower candlesticks
soft mold, one has hairline to stem, black paper label on both, 4 1/4″ by 3 3/4″ each.
$500-$600/pair

Sunflower shouldered low bowl
burst bubble to one leaf, unmarked, 4″ by 7 1/4″.
$400-$475

Sunflower jardinière
with very strong mold and color, two tiny repairs at rim, two flecks to the leaves on body, unmarked, 13″ by 16″.
$2,200-$2,400

Sunflower jardinière and pedestal
with excellent mold and color, restoration to chip at rim of jardinière, a few small flecks, unmarked; jardinière: 10 1/2″ tall; pedestal: 18 1/2″ tall.
$4,200-$4,300

Sunflower jardinière
with crisp mold and good color, minute nick to base of one stem, unmarked, 8″ by 11″.
$1,000-$1,200

Sunflower jardinière
with crisp mold, opposing cracks and several small chips, unmarked, 8 1/2″ by 11″.
$375-$425

Sunflower four-sided planter
unmarked, rare, 3 3/4″ by 11″.

$1,000-$1,200

Sunflower bulbous vase
with collared rim, soft mold, unmarked, 9 1/4″ by 6 3/4″.

$1,200-$1,400

Sunflower bulbous vase
with good color, small burst to decoration and nick to foot ring (does not show on side), unmarked, 5 1/4″ by 5″.

$450-$550

Sunflower bulbous vase
with restoration to chip at rim, unmarked, 8 1/4″ by 6 1/2″.

$700-$800

Sunflower bulbous vase
excellent mold and color, unmarked, 8 1/4″ by 6 1/2″.

$1,100-$1,300

Sunflower bulbous vase
with strong mold and good color, tight 1″ bruise to rim, unmarked, 9 1/2″ tall.

$1,400-$1,600

Sunflower flaring vase
good mold, unmarked, 7 1/4″ by 5″.

$900-$1,000

Sunflower ovoid vase
excellent mold and color, unmarked, 10 1/4″ by 6 1/4″.

$2,000-$2,200

Sunflower spherical vase
remnant of black paper label, 6 1/4″ by 7 1/2″.
$800-$900

Sunflower two-handled vase
unmarked, 5″ tall.
$375-$425

Two Sunflower two-handled vases
soft mold to both, one has restoration to body chip and rim chip, unmarked, 5 1/4″ by 4 1/4″ and 6″ by 5″.
$650-$750/pair

Sunflower two-handled vessel
unmarked, 5 1/4″ by 4 1/4″.
$500-$600

Sylvan

A rustic pattern from the first quarter of the 20th century, Sylvan pieces featured textured surfaces in colors of brown, tan, and muddy green, with leafy decoration, and some animal motifs, including hunting dogs, a fox and chickens, birds, and squirrels. Interiors are usually a glossy green. All are unmarked.

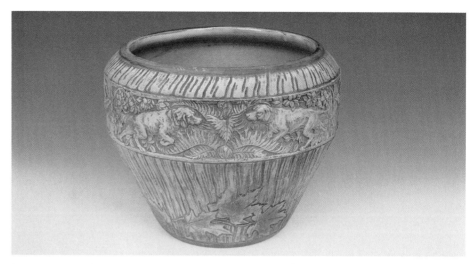

Sylvan jardinière
decorated with hunting dogs, with olive-green glossy glazed interior, unmarked, 10″ by 12 1/2″.
$1,500-$1,600

Sylvan umbrella stand
(750-21″) with olive-green glossy glazed interior, unmarked, with rim chip, 21 1/2″ by 10″.
$700-$800

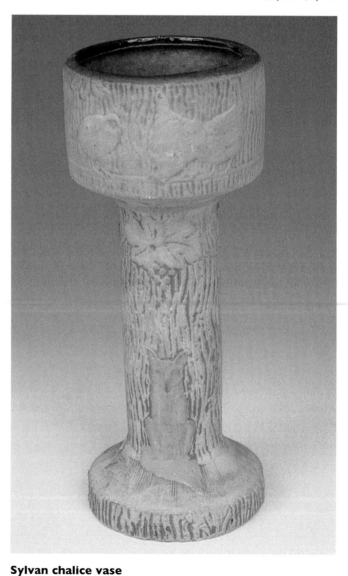

Sylvan chalice vase
decorated with fox and chickens, with olive-green glossy glazed interior, unmarked, 9 1/2″ by 4″.
$600-$700

Teasel

The stylized plant form on Teasel (1938) is usually covered in dripping or blended glazes of dusty blue or pink, ivory, brown, and even sea foam green, sometimes set off by metallic accents. Pieces usually have impressed marks.

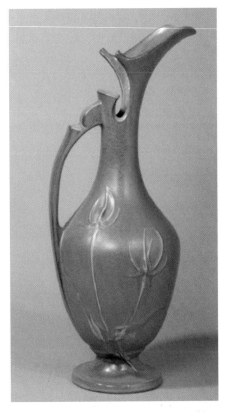

Teasel blue ewer
(890-18″), impressed mark.

$500-$600

Teasel spherical vessel
(343-6″) with small nick to one flower, impressed mark.

$150-$175

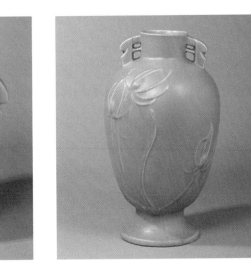

Teasel blue bulbous vase
(884-8″), impressed mark.

$175-$200

Teasel sea foam bulbous vase
(889-15″), impressed mark.

$500-$600

Teasel blue flaring urn
(888-12″), impressed mark.

$375-$425

Teasel beige basket
(349-10˝), unmarked.

$250-$275

Two Teasel pieces
blue footed vessel (881-6˝) and a corseted beige vase (887-7˝), impressed mark.

$325-$350/pair

Two Teasel vases
(881-6˝ and 882-6˝), one pink and one blue, impressed mark.

$300-$350/pair

Pair of flaring Teasel vases
(886-9˝), one pink and one beige, impressed mark.

$300-$350/pair

Thorn Apple

Introduced in 1937, Thorn Apple has a tapering blossom on one side of the vessel and a thorny pod on the other. Background colors are blue fading to turquoise, brown to tan with yellow accents, and green with a salmon pink. Pieces usually have impressed marks.

Thorn Apple blue vase
small chip to base, marked, 10″ tall.

$150-$200

Thorn Apple brown hanging basket
tight 1″ line to one hole, unmarked, 5 3/4″ by 7 1/2″.

$225-$275

Three Thorn Apple brown pieces
triple candleholder (1120) and pair of cornucopia-shaped vases (127-6″), a couple of tiny flecks to one, impressed marks.

$200-$250/set

Two Thorn Apple brown pieces
wall pocket (1280-8″) with clay pimple to body and vase (810-6″) with minute fleck to handle, impressed marks.

$400-$450/pair

Thorn Apple pink pedestal
unmarked, 17″.

$275-$325

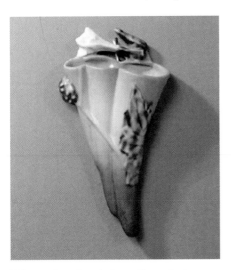

Thorn Apple pink wall pocket
unmarked, 9 1/4″ tall.

$450-$550

Two Thorn Apple pieces
brown pillow vase (812-6″) and pink bowl (307-6″), both marked.

$250-$300/pair

Two Thorn Apple pieces
pink squat vase (808-4″) with bruise to rim and
blue bulbous vase (818-8″), impressed marks.
$200-$250/pair

**Three Thorn
Apple pieces**
 including a pair of
green candlesticks and
pink vase (808-4″), all
marked (obscured on
candlesticks); candlesticks:
2 1/2″ tall.

$325-$375/set

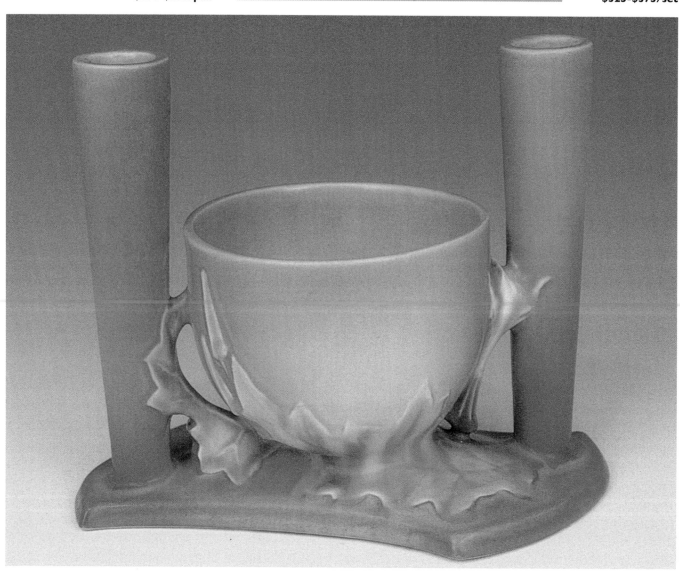

Thorn Apple blue centerpiece
impressed mark 312, 6 1/2″ by 7 1/2″ by 4″.
$350-$450

Topeo

A generally bulbous line from 1934, Topeo has symmetrical tapering garlands that look like small cabbages in certain glaze combinations. Often found in blue-green turquoise, there is also a blood red. Pieces are unmarked or have a foil label.

Topeo blue bowl
unmarked, 4″ by 9 1/4″.

$200-$250

Topeo blue console set
silver foil label on bowl; bowl: 4 1/4″ by 12 3/4″, candlesticks: 4″ tall.

$500-$600

Two Topeo blue pieces
squat center bowl and ovoid vase; short tight line to rim of vase, unmarked; 11″ diameter and 6 3/4″ by 4″.

$300-$350/pair

Topeo blue tapering vase
unmarked, 8 1/2″ tall.

$450-$550

Topeo blue bulbous vessel
unmarked, 9 1/2″ by 5 1/2″.

$450-$550

Topeo blue spherical vessel
unmarked, 6 1/4″ by 7″.

$350-$400

Topeo red low bowl
unmarked, 2 3/4″ by 8 1/4″.

$90-$110

Topeo red spherical vessel
silver foil label, 6 1/2″ by 7″.

$175-$225

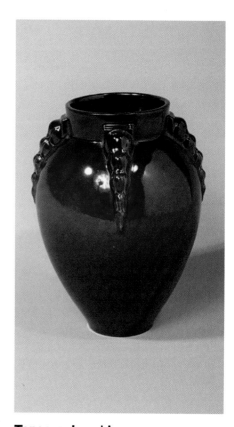

Topeo red ovoid vase
with very strong mold, unmarked, 9 1/4″ by 6 3/4″.

$300-$350

Topeo red vase
(657-6 3/4″), unmarked.

$200-$250

Topeo red (sometimes called "Mowaˊ) bulbous vase and Artcraft red planter;
some scratches and flecks to both, 1″ crack to base of planter, foil label to one, 7″ and 4″ tall.

$90-$110/pair

Tourist

Part of the creamwares, Tourist pieces date to about 1910 and feature a wide banded motif showing touring cars on a day in the country. Pieces are unmarked.

Tourist bowl
3″ by 5 1/2″.

$2,400-$2,500

Tourist pedestal
3/4″ tight line to rim (in making?) and very minor losses to paint, unmarked, 21 1/2″ tall by 11″ diameter at base.

$2,100-$2,300

Tourist planter or window box
minor paint flaking, 6 7/8″ by 7 7/8″ by 13″.

$2,500-$3,000

Tourist jardinière
unmarked, 7 1/4″ by 8 1/2″.

$2,200-$2,400

Tourist trumpet vase
unmarked, 7 3/4″ by 5″.

$1,500-$1,700

Tourmaline

Introduced in 1933, Tourmaline has a distinctive ribbed band on many of its pieces and a mottled dripping glaze combination that includes blue, ivory, tan, turquoise, raspberry, and amber-yellow. Pieces are unmarked or have a foil label.

Two Tourmaline pieces
shouldered jardinière and four-sided planter with ribbed base, unmarked, 5″ and 6 1/4″ tall.
$225-$250/pair

Two Tourmaline pieces
shouldered jardinière and tall faceted vase embossed with circles, covered in a mottled blue-green glaze, one has foil label, 5″ and 10 1/4″ tall.
$450-$500/pair

Two Tourmaline blue pieces
bulbous urn and corseted footed vase embossed with rings (restoration to base), one has foil label, 6 1/2″ and 8 1/4″ tall.
$150-$175/pair

Four Tourmaline vases
in either mottled turquoise, mottled gold, mottled pink and blue, or yellow and blue crystalline glaze, one marked with silver foil label, 5 3/4″ by 6 1/4″ each.
$300-$350/set

Two spherical vases
Tourmaline and turquoise Matt Color, foil labels, 5 1/4″ and 3 1/4″ tall.
$350-$450/pair

Pair of Tourmaline bulbous vases
one blue, one orange; blue vase has chip at rim, both unmarked, 5 3/4″ by 6 1/4″ each.
$110-$140/pair

Two Tourmaline pieces
bulbous vase (line and large repaired chip to rim) and a cornucopia-shaped vase (several very minor grinding chips), both unmarked; taller: 7 1/2″.
$125-$150/pair

Tourmaline blue two-handled bulbous vase
minor grinding chips and abrasions, foil label, 5 3/4″ by 6 1/4″.
$110-$140

Tourmaline vase
unmarked, 7 1/2″ by 3 1/2″.
$250-$300

Tourmaline blue vessel
gold foil label, 6 3/8″ by 4 3/4″.

$175-$225

Two Tourmaline blue bulbous vessels
one has 2 1/2″ crack from rim, unmarked, 7 1/2″ by 6 1/4″ each.
$250-$300/pair

Tourmaline blue spherical vessel
unmarked, 5 1/4″ by 6 1/4″.

$125-$175

Two Tourmaline vases
twisted faceted (restoration to rim chip) and flaring (small chip to top), both covered in a mottled pink and blue matte glaze, unmarked, both 8 1/4″ tall.
$150-$175/pair

Tuscany

From the mid-1920s, Tuscany has a mottled glaze on classically shaped vessels, and handles in the shape of grape clusters and leaves. Pink is more common than gray. Pieces are unmarked or have a paper label.

Tuscany footed bowl
black label, 6 1/4″ by 4 1/8″.

$150-$170

Tuscany pink candleholder
unmarked, 3 7/8″ by 3 7/8″.

$50-$70

Two Tuscany pink pieces
footed bowl (some short tight lines to rim) and bulbous vase (restorations to rim and base), unmarked, 9 3/4″ diameter and 8 3/4″ by 7″.

$100-$150/pair

Two Tuscany pink flowerpots and under plates
several hairlines and chips to larger pot, minor chips to smaller, unmarked; taller: 6 1/2″.

$110-$140/pair

Tuscany pink squat vessel
spider lines to base, unmarked, 5 1/2″ by 7″.

$75-$85

Two Tuscany wall pockets
one gray and one pink, chip to hole on both, unmarked, 8 1/2″ and 7 1/2″ tall.

$225-$250/pair

Utility Ware

Made over two decades until the 1940s, these simple bowls and pitchers had a wide band of solid color accented by black or gray pinstripes. A few examples have hand-painted flowers or landscapes, and others have stylized leaves. Pieces feature the "Rv" ink stamp.

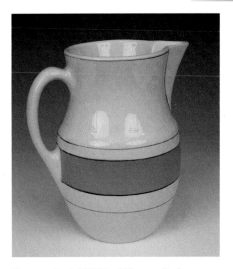

Decorated Utility Ware pitcher
with blue stripe, "Rv" ink stamp, 8" tall.
$175-$200

Decorated Utility Ware mixing bowl
with green stripe, "Rv" ink stamp, 9" diameter.
$125-$150

Three decorated Utility Ware bowls
11" diameter mixing bowl with blue stripe, 10" bake pan with gray stripe, and 9" mixing bowl with orange stripe; several scratches and some nicks overall, "Rv" ink stamps.
$125-$175/set

Four decorated Utility Ware pieces
three bowls and pitcher painted with stripes; small chip to pitcher and some hairlines to smallest bowl, "Rv" ink stamps; largest: 6" by 9 1/2"
$200-$250/set

Four decorated Utility Ware pitchers
a few nicks and scratches overall, dark crazing to one, "Rv" ink stamps; tallest: 7 1/2".
$225-$275/set

Velmoss

The Velmoss name is associated with three distinct Roseville lines, two of which are described here. The early Velmoss has an Arts & Crafts aura and is a dull green or tan blend with large stylized vertical leaves cloaking the vessels. Pieces are unmarked.
Velmoss II (1935) has naturalistic leaves draped over a wavy ridged border with background colors of muted greens, blues, and pinks. Pieces occasionally feature impressed marks, but are mostly unmarked or have a foil label.

Early Velmoss jardinière
some minor flakes, unmarked, 12″ by 16″.
$1,350-$1,450

Early Velmoss jardinière
unmarked, 7″ tall.
$650-$750

Early Velmoss bulbous vase
with flared mouth (129-8″), 8″ tall.
$900-$1,000

Early Velmoss jardinière
unmarked, 7″ tall.
$800-$900

Early Velmoss cylindrical vase
unmarked, 8 1/4″ by 2 1/2″.

$400-$500

Early Velmoss cylindrical vase
glaze fleck to one leaf, unmarked, 9″ tall.

$500-$600

Velmoss II bulbous vase
1/2″ touch-up to rim, unmarked, 12 1/4″ by 6 1/4″.

$150-$175

Two Velmoss II green pieces
fan vase (934-8″?) and faceted planter with
restoration to one corner, faint impressed mark to
one; planter: 3 1/2″ by 11″.

$150-$200/pair

Velmoss II pink vase
gold foil label, 14 1/4″ by 8 3/4″.

$600-$700

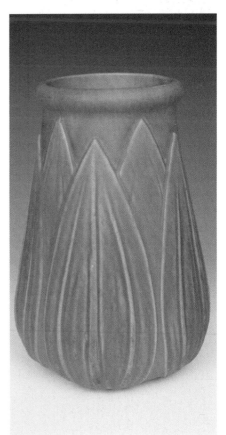

Early Velmoss tapering vase
(136-10″), unmarked, 10″ tall.

$900-$1,000

Two Velmoss II double bud vases
one green and one blue, blue has silver foil label, 8
1/4″ by 5″ and 8 3/4″ by 7 1/4″.

$250-$350/pair

Two Velmoss II vases
one blue and one pink, unmarked, 6 1/4″ by 5 3/4″
and 7 1/4″ by 5 1/2″.

$400-$500/pair

Velmoss Scroll

Dating from just before 1920, and once known as Velmoss I, this highly stylized design has a pattern of roses, leaves, and stems on a cream body. Pieces are unmarked.

Velmoss Scroll hanging basket
with 3″ line from rim and 2″ line to bottom, unmarked, 7 1/2″ tall.

$200-$250

Velmoss Scroll console set
consisting of flaring footed bowl (strong mold, restored chip to rim) and pair of tall candlesticks, unmarked; bowl: 5″ by 9″, sticks: 8 1/4″ tall.

$250-$300/set

Two Velmoss Scroll vases
one corseted (1/4″ chip to base) and one cylindrical bud, unmarked, 10″ and 6 1/4″ tall.

$275-$325/pair

Velmoss Scroll wall pocket
with 2″ hairline to rim, short line to front, unmarked, 11″.

$125-$150

Velmoss Scroll wall pocket
with small chip to back corner, unmarked, 11 1/2″ tall.

$200-$250

Venetian Line

Originally made around the turn of the 19th century, these utilitarian cooking wares came in a buff color, pale yellow, or with a robin's egg blue glaze. They have an embossed saw-tooth pattern and are usually marked. Later examples may also be found.

Venetian ovenware bowl
came with wire handle and wooden grip, impressed indistinct mark, 8 1/4″ by 4 1/8″.
$80-$100

Venetian ovenware bowl
in blue glaze, came with wire handle and wooden grip, impressed mark "Venetian Fireproof," 10 3/4″ by 5 1/8″.
$200-$250

Miniature Venetian ovenware bowl
with wire handle and wooden grip, possibly a salesman's sample, impressed mark "Venetian," 3 1/2″ diameter by 1 5/8″ without handle.
No established value.

Victorian Art Pottery

From the mid-1920s and with more than a little art nouveau influence, this line often bears a stylized band of birds and leaves with glazes in dull brown, tan, and black. A very few have bright vivid colors. Pieces are usually unmarked or have an "Rv" ink stamp or foil label.

Victorian Art Pottery bulbous vase
restoration to drill hole on bottom, foil label, 9 1/2″ by 9 1/2″.
$350-$400

Brown Victorian Art Pottery bulbous vessel
small nick to base, unmarked, 4 1/4″ by 6″.
$200-$225

Two Victorian Art Pottery pieces
yellow bulbous vessel with line to rim and
small blue jardinière with various minor chips,
unmarked, 5 1/4″ by 7 1/4″ and 4 1/4″ by 6″.
$300-$350/pair

Two Victorian Art Pottery vessels
in typical brown and tan colors: left, 258-7″, unmarked, $350 to $400; right, 132-4″, with "Rv" ink stamp.
$300-$350

Vista

The design of this line has prompted
some to call it "Forest" because the
lower half of the vessels look like tree
trunks set in a watery landscape, but
the top half of the vessels are clearly
large-petal flowers that continue
in an unbroken vista. Hues are a
wet, watercolor green, lavender, and
burgundy on a gray background. Pieces
are usually unmarked or ink stamped in
rare instances.

Vista basket
unmarked, 6 3/4″ by 4 3/4″.
$450-$550

Vista basket
short line to handle, rare, 8 1/2″ by 6″.
$650-$750

Vista hanging basket
firing lines to two handles, bruise to rim, and
shallow spider line to base does not go through,
unmarked, 3 1/2″ by 6 3/4″.
$200-$250

Vista bowl
several chips to base, bruise and flecks to rim,
unmarked, 6 3/4″ diameter.
$150-$200

Vista low bowl
good color and mold, stamped 246, 3 1/4″ by 7″.
$175-$225

Vista bowl
minute fleck at rim and base, unmarked, 4″ by
8 1/4″.
$225-$275

Vista jardinière
some burst bubbles, unmarked, 6 1/2″ by 7″.
$275-$325

Vista jardinière and pedestal
in as-is condition (chips, cracks, etc.), unmarked;
pedestal: 18″ tall, jardinière: 8 1/2″ by 10″.
$300-$350

Vista jardinière
small chip to rim, unmarked, 9 3/4″ tall.
$325-$375

Vista jardinière
fleck to base ring, very minor abrasions, some
burst bubbles overall, unmarked, 8 1/4″ by 9 1/4″.
$325-$375

Vista bulbous vase
with buttressed handles at rim, short tight line and
repaired chip at rim, some pinhead sized flecks to
body, unmarked, 9 3/4″ by 5 1/4″.
$425-$475

Vista jardinière
long line and minor burst to rim, 9 1/2″ by 10 3/4″.
$300-$350

Vista jardinière
some minor nicks, unmarked, 10 1/2″ tall.
$650-$750

Vista bulbous vase
unmarked, 17 1/2˝ by 7 1/2˝.

$1,500-$1,700

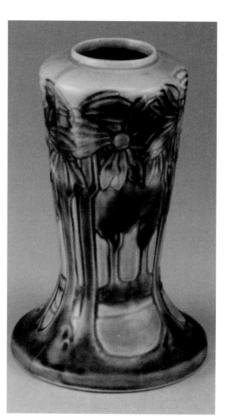

Vista footed vase
unmarked, 10˝ by 6 1/4˝.

$600-$700

Vista vase
several lines from rim, a couple of small chips at
base, unmarked, 14 1/2˝ by 4 1/4˝.

$650-$750

Vista rectangular planter
peppering to rim and some minor nicks,
unmarked, rare, 6 1/4˝ by 11 1/2˝.

$1,300-$1,500

Vista wall pocket
some small chips and nicks, unmarked, 8 3/4˝.

$450-$550

Vista tapering vase
long tight line from rim, 15˝ by 6˝.

$900-$1,000

Vista floor vase/umbrella stand
some minor flecks, unmarked, 20˝ by 9 1/2˝.

$1,600-$1,800

Water Lily

The large flowers and lily pads on this line from 1943 float on a textured surface that resembles rippling water. Background colors are blue, brown, and pink, while the lily blossoms can be white, yellow, or lavender. Most pieces have raised marks.

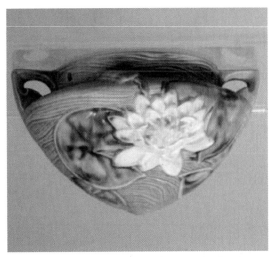

Water Lily blue hanging basket
stamped "USA," 5 1/2" by 8 3/4".

$200-$225

Water Lily blue cookie jar
(1-8"), raised mark, 9" by 10 1/4".

$400-$500

Water Lily brown cookie jar
(1-8"), strong mold, raised mark.

$400-$450

Two Water Lily brown pieces
bulbous planter (663-5") with chip to one handle and corseted vase (80-10"), raised marks.

$110-$140/pair

Three Water Lily pieces
blue vase (78-9˝), brown jardinière (437-4˝), and pink vase (71-4˝) with repair to rim, all marked.

$200-$250/set

Water Lily pink cookie jar
(1-8˝), pinhead-sized fleck to edge of rim and touch-up to nick and burst bubble on flower, raised mark.

$300-$400

Water Lily pink ewer
(12-15˝), repair to crack at spout and touch-up to one flower, raised mark.

$175-$225

Water Lily pink bulbous vase
(79-9˝), small bruise to petal, raised mark.

$110-$140

White Rose

This line from 1940 features large blossoms on textured two-tone backgrounds of blue-turquoise, green-brown, and pink-green. Pieces feature raised marks.

Pair of White Rose blue book-shaped bookends
(7), restoration to tip of flower and to corners of one, and restoration to three corners of other, raised marks, 4 3/4″ by 5″ by 4 3/4″.
$125-$175/pair

Two White Rose pieces
blue spherical jardinière (653-4″) with opposing lines to rim and pink vase (976), raised marks; vase: 4 1/4″ by 3 1/4″.
$110-$140/pair

White Rose blue ewer/pitcher
(990-10″), raised mark, large base chip, 10″ by 7″ by 7″.
$175-$200

White Rose blue tea set
(1), raised marks; teapot: 7″ by 8 1/4″.
$300-$350/set

Two White Rose blue pieces
flat vase (987-9″) with dark crazing lines and fleck to one flower and bulbous vase (974-6″), raised marks.
$125-$175/pair

Pair of large White Rose blue bulbous vases
(991-12″), nick and fleck to one, short tight line to rim of the other, raised marks.

$275-$325/pair

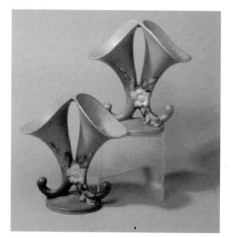

Two White Rose double cornucopia vases
one pink and one blue (145-8″) hairline around base of pink one raised marks.

$150-$200/pair

Pair of White Rose vases
one blue and one pink (980-6″), raised marks.

$250-$300/pair •

Two White Rose pieces
brown planter (387-4″) with several chips to base and large blue bowl (394-14″), both marked.

$125-$175/pair

White Rose blue floor vase
(994-16″) with restoration to chips at rim, raised mark.

$250-$300

White Rose brown jardinière
(653-6″), underglaze bruise to base, raised mark.

$110-$140

White Rose brown pitcher
(990-10″), tight crack near spout, raised mark.

$90-$110

White Rose brown bulbous vase
(992-15″), good mold, raised mark.

$375-$425

White Rose brown pillow vase
(984-8″) with strong mold, raised mark.

$150-$200

White Rose brown bulbous vase
(978-4″), raised mark, 4 1/4″ by 3 1/4″.

$175-$225

Three White Rose pieces
brown bud vase (995-7″), small pink jardinière (653-4″), and pink bulbous vase (986-9″), raised marks.

$175-$225/set

Two White Rose brown pieces
pillow vase (984-8″) and tall vase (992-15″); flat 1/2 inch chip to bottom ring, restoration to two bruises at rim, and 4″ tight line to base of larger vase, raised marks.

$225-$275/pair

White Rose green basket
(363-10″), raised mark.

$250-$300

White Rose pink basket
(363-10˝), raised mark.

$250-$300

White Rose pink ewer
(993-15˝), small fleck to one petal, raised mark.

$250-$300

White Rose green asymmetrical two-handled vase
(982-7˝), raised mark, 7˝ by 7 3/8˝ by 4 7/8˝.

$225-$275

White Rose pink jardinière
(656-10˝) and pedestal set, 1/4˝ chip to jardinière, both marked.

$700-$800

White Rose pink tea set
(1) with small glaze scale to petal of teapot, raised marks; teapot: 7 1/2˝ by 8 3/4˝.

$300-$350/set

White Rose pink urn
(991-12˝), raised mark.

$175-$225

Three White Rose pieces

pink urn (146-6˝), small bulbous pink vase (978-4˝) with peppering and chip to inner rim, and blue vase (982-7˝), raised marks.

$150-$200/set

Two White Rose wall pockets

one pink (1289-8˝) with minor firing flake near tip, and one brown (1288-6˝), raised marks.

$450-$500/pair

White Rose pink vase

(978-4˝), raised mark, 4 1/4˝ by 3 1/4˝.

$90-$110

Three White Rose pieces

pink cornucopia-shaped vase (144-8˝), flaring vase (980-6˝), and blue bowl (391-10˝) with chips to rim and base, all marked.

$150-$200/set

Five White Rose pieces

pink bowl (394-14˝) with small chip; pair of pink candlesticks (1142-4 1/2˝), one reglued, the other with flat chip to base; blue cornucopia vase and built-in frog (1) with bruise to berry; and pink cornucopia vase, all marked.

$225-$275/set

Wincraft

This line from 1948, with sleek designs and bright colors under a glossy finish, was named for then-company president Robert Windisch. There is really no consistent trait to these pieces other than the sheen. The company borrowed design elements from earlier lines and favored colors like chartreuse, apricot, and azure blue. Pieces usually have raised marks.

Trial matte glaze Wincraft flaring footed vase
decorated with arrowroot plant on a shaded yellow and red ground (2V2-10″), raised mark with glaze codes, 10 1/4″ by 5 1/2″.

$750

Wincraft brown hanging basket
with ivy, unmarked, 6 1/4″ by 6″.

$90-$110

Wincraft candleholders
of elongated shape (252), raised mark, each 5 3/4″ by 2 3/4″ by 2 1/8″.

$90-$110/pair

Wincraft blue coffee set
(250) with minor fleck to spout of creamer, raised marks; coffee pot: 9 3/4″ by 8″.

$300-$350/set

Wincraft center bowl
(226-8″), raised mark, 10 1/4″ by 8 1/2″ by 2 3/4″

$150-$175

Wincraft brown coffee set
(250) decorated with berries, raised marks; coffee pot: 9 1/2″ by 7 3/4″.

$350-$450/set

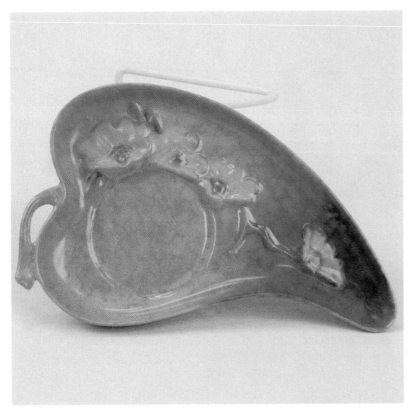

Wincraft leaf-shaped dish
with cup ring, impressed mark and obscured number, 8 1/4″ by 5 3/8″ by 1 1/8″.
$90-$110

Two four-sided Wincraft jars
(274-7″), one brown and one green, raised marks.
$250-$300/pair

Wincraft brown tea set
(271) with minor underglaze flake to base of creamer, raised marks; teapot: 7″ by 9 1/2″.

$175-$200/set

Three Wincraft pieces

two blue vases, one with pine cone (2V2-8″) and the other with tulip (282-8″), and yellow vase with small white blossoms and leaves (273-8″), raised marks.

$200-$250/set

Five Wincraft pieces

yellow vase with white rose (241-6″), nick; yellow bud vase (273-8″) with small chip to base; yellow bowl (227-10″); blue vase with pine cone (272-6″); and blue basket (209-12″) with grapes, all marked.

$225-$275/set

Wincraft blue flaring vase

(2V2-8″) on squat base, with pinecone, raised mark.

$90-$110

Two Wincraft blue pieces

tall vase (263-14″) and basket (208-8″), both decorated with blossoms and leaves, raised marks.

$350-$450/pair

Two Wincraft blue pieces

vase (284-10″) and basket (208-8″), raised marks.

$225-$275/pair

Wincraft brown hanging basket

with ivy, unmarked, 6 1/4″ by 6″.

$250-$300

Wincraft yellow footed dish

with leaves and berries (228-12″), raised mark, 15 1/2″ by 5 1/4″ by 4 7/8″.

$120-$140

Two Wincraft pieces

brown wall pocket (267-5″) with ivy and long yellow footed dish with leaves and berries (228-12″), raised marks.

$175-$225/pair

Wincraft three-piece tea set

comprised of sugar dish (271S), creamer (271C), and teapot (271P), minor nick to inner lid, raised marks; teapot: 6 3/4″ tall.

$110-$140/set

Wincraft cylindrical panther vase

(290-11″), 2″ hairline from rim, small flat chip to bottom, raised mark.

$350-$400

Wincraft ikebana vase

(1055-9″), minute flecks to base, raised mark.

$110-$140

Wincraft flaring vase

(275-12″) with thistle on yellow/amber mottled ground, raised mark.

$300-$400

Wincraft green tea set

(271) with small bruise to handle of sugar bowl, raised marks; teapot: 6 3/4″ by 9 1/4″.

$175-$200/set

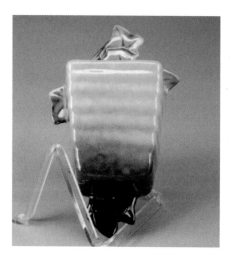

Wincraft wall pocket

(266-5″), minute nick to back of hanging hole, raised mark.

$150-$200

Wincraft floor vase with buttressed base

(289-18″) with ivory roses on a mottled vermillion ground, small 1/2″ chip under the base, raised mark.

$400-$500

Wincraft vase

(288-15″), painted over nick to one leaf, raised mark.

$150-$200

Wincraft brown four-sided vase

(274-7″) with panels of blowing wind, a couple of very minor nicks, raised mark.

$110-$140

Wincraft wall pocket

with ivy on a blue ground (267-5″), raised mark.

$150-$200

Wincraft yellow pillow vase

with pine cone (272-6″), raised mark.

$65-$75

Windsor

Introduced in 1931, Windsor featured mottled glazes of muted blue and orange, decorated with floral motifs that were either stylized or impressionistic; some also have geometric patterns. Pieces are unmarked or have a foil label.

Windsor diamond-shaped center bowl
decorated with green oak leaves and acorns, minor burst bubble to tip of one handle, unmarked, 2 1/4″ by 16″.

$350-$400

Windsor blue low bowl
black paper label, 3″ by 9 1/2″.

$250-$300

Windsor blue bulbous urn
impressed with stylized floral design in green and yellow, foil label, 5 1/4″ by 4 3/4″.

$375-$425

Windsor spherical lamp base impressed
with green ferns on a mottled blue ground, drilled, 1″ glaze scaling to handle, unmarked; pottery: 7″ by 7 1/4″.

$550-$650

Windsor blue bulbous vessel
impressed with geometric pattern around neck in
yellow and green, unmarked, 6 1/4″ by 6 1/4″.
$400-$500

Windsor orange diamond-shaped center bowl
crisply decorated with green oak leaves and acorns, restoration to one handle, unmarked, 2 1/4″ by 16″.
$150-$200

Windsor orange squat low bowl
with impressed decoration of stylized green leaves and peas, flower frog, 1/2″ chip to base of flower frog, foil
label to one; bowl: 2 3/4″ by 12″.
$200-$250

Windsor gourd-shaped urn
decorated with green fern, foil label, 9 1/4″ by 6
1/4″.

$1,300-$1,500

Windsor orange vase
decorated with green geometric pattern around
neck, black label, 6 1/4″ by 6 1/4″.

$375-$400

Windsor orange trumpet vase
impressed with abstract pattern in green,
unmarked, 7 1/4″ by 4 1/2″.

$450-$500

Wisteria

Wisteria from 1937 features large pink or lavender hanging blooms and leaves on a textured surface. Though collectors typically refer to blue or brown pieces, both colors can be found on the same piece, with one dominating, accented by yellow or green. Pieces are unmarked or have foil labels.

Wisteria blue hanging basket
with strong mold, some nicks and flecks, two opposing hairlines, chip to both handles, unmarked, 4 1/2″ by 7 1/2″.

$400-$500

Wisteria blue jardinière
with strong mold and color, opposing cracks from rim, a chip to both handles, 7″ by 9″.

$200-$250

Wisteria blue bottle-shaped vase
with excellent mold and color, bruise to rim, unmarked, 15″ by 7 1/2″.

$2,100-$2,300

Wisteria blue bulbous vase
minute fleck to rim, gold foil label, 8 1/4″ by 6 1/4″.

$1,100-$1,300

Wisteria blue cylindrical two-handled vase
strong mold and color, minor nick to petal, unmarked, 10 1/4″ by 6 1/4″.

$900-$1,200

Wisteria blue flaring vase
with strong mold, unmarked, 8 1/4″.

$700-$800

Wisteria blue gourd-shaped vase
foil label, 7 1/2″ by 5 1/2″.

$900-$1,000

Wisteria blue vessel
(632-5″), bruise and factory clay separation at rim, unmarked, 5″ by 6″.

$275-$325

Wisteria blue spherical vessel
with excellent mold and color, restoration to 10˝ line going through base, unmarked, 6 1/2˝ by 8 1/2˝.
$400-$450

Wisteria blue wall pocket
with strong mold and color, unmarked, 8 1/2˝ by 7˝.
$1,650-$1,750

Two Wisteria squat vessels
one brown and one blue, both unmarked, both 4 1/4˝ by 6 1/4˝.
$550-$650/pair

Wisteria brown four-sided planter
with good mold, unmarked, 3 1/4˝ by 12˝.
$350-$400

Pair of Wisteria brown candlesticks
unmarked, 4 3/4˝ by 4 3/4˝.
$350-$400/pair

Wisteria brown bulbous jardinière
good mold and color, unmarked, 5 1/4˝ by 6 3/4˝.
$350-$400

Pair of Wisteria bulbous vases
one brown (minute fleck to one handle) and one blue (good mold and color), unmarked, each 6 1/4˝ by 4˝.
$750-$850/pair

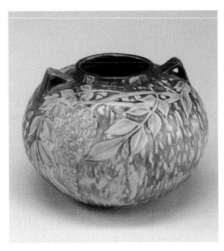

Wisteria brown bulbous vase
nick to body and minor bruise to one flower,
unmarked, 6 3/4″ by 8″.

$450-$550

Wisteria brown jardinière and pedestal
several tight cracks through base and minor
bruise to one flower of jardinière; pedestal mint,
unmarked; jardinière: 10″ tall; pedestal: 18″ tall.

$1,700-$1,900

Wisteria brown bottle-shaped vase
with two handles, unmarked, 9 1/4″ by 5 3/4″.

$450-$550

Wisteria brown gourd-shaped vase
foil label, 7″ by 6″.

$400-$450

Wisteria brown ovoid vase
short line inside rim, possible scaling in
manufacture, unmarked, 6″ tall.

$350-$400

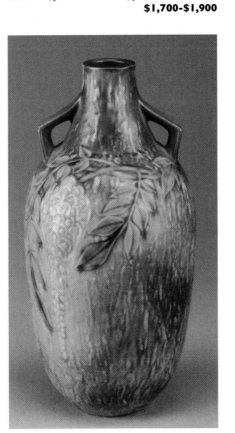

Wisteria brown bottle-shaped vase
foil label, 15 1/4″ tall.

$1,600-$1,800

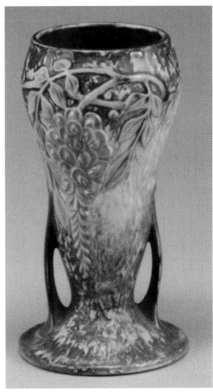

Wisteria brown flaring vase
crisp mold and good color, unmarked, 8 1/4″ by 4
1/2″.

$450-$550

Pair of Wisteria pear-shaped vessels
one brown and one blue; good mold and color of blue one, minute glaze fleck near base of brown one, gold foil label on one, both 6 1/4″ by 4 1/4″.
$750-$850/pair

Wisteria brown corseted two-handled vase
with strong mold and color, 1/2″ chip with bruise to one handle, gold foil label, 10 1/2″ by 8″.
$450-$500

Two Wisteria vases
one brown squat with fleck to decoration and one small blue planter with line and 1/2″ chip to rim, both unmarked, 4 1/4″ tall each.
$350-$400/pair

Wisteria brown tapering vase
unmarked, 10 1/2″ tall.
$900-$1,000

Wisteria brown two-handled classically shaped vessel
with strong mold and color, two small glaze flakes at base, unmarked, 8 1/4″ by 7 1/2″.
$400-$450

Wisteria brown spherical vessel
with closed-in rim, unmarked, 5 1/2″ by 6 1/4″.
$325-$400

Wisteria brown squat vessel
with good mold and color, gold foil label, 4 1/2″ by 5 3/4″.
$300-$400

Zephyr Lily

This line from 1946 features blossoms of white, yellow, rose, and lavender (often two bloom colors on the same piece) on a textured background that looks like a pool rippling with raindrops. Body colors are variegated blues, browns, and greens. Pieces have raised marks.

Zephyr Lily blue basket
(393-7˝) with chip at base, raised mark.
$110-$140

Zephyr Lily blue hanging basket
marked "U.S.A.," 5 1/2˝ by 7˝.
$200-$250

Zephyr Lily blue hanging basket
marked "U.S.A.," 6˝ by 7 1/2˝.
$125-$175

Zephyr Lily blue floor vase
(142-18˝), restoration to small chips on handles, raised mark.
$450-$500

Zephyr Lily blue pillow vase
(205-6˝), 7˝ by 6 1/2˝ by 2 3/8˝.
$250-$300

Pair of Zephyr Lily vases
(136-9˝), one with line from rim, raised marks.
$150-$200/pair

Two Zephyr Lily pieces
blue vase (137-10˝) with flaring rim (1/4˝ chip at rim) and brown pillow vase (205-6˝) with a couple of shallow scratches to base, raised marks.
$110-$140/pair

Three Zephyr Lily pieces
blue flaring vase (136-9″) with nick to base
and pair of brown bookends (16), all marked;
bookends: 5 1/4″ tall each.

$225-$275/pair

Zephyr Lily blue wall pocket
(1297-8″), small flakes to base.

$150-$200

Zephyr Lily brown basket
(393-7″), raised mark, 7 3/8″ by 6 1/8″ by 5″.

$200-$250

Zephyr Lily brown hanging
basket, unmarked, 5 1/2″ by 8″.

$200-$250

Zephyr Lily candleholders
(1163-4 1/2″), raised marks, chip to one rim, 4 7/8″ by 3 3/4″.

$80-$90/pair

Zephyr Lily brown cookie jar
(5-8″), chip to one flower and small chips
to lid rim, raised mark.

$300-$350

Zephyr Lily brown jardinière
(671-8″), firing bruise to base and a few small
flecks to high points, raised mark.

$225-$275

Zephyr Lily brown tea set
(7) with small burst bubble to creamer, raised marks; teapot: 7″ by 9 1/4″.

$350-$450/set

Three Zephyr Lily brown pieces
flowerpot (672-5″), vase (132-7″) with small filled-in chip to rim, and center bowl (476-10″), all marked.

$175-$225/set

Zephyr Lily green jardinière
(671-8″) and pedestal, a few minor flecks to rim and body, raised mark to jardinière and "U.S.A." mark to pedestal.

$450-$500

Zephyr Lily ewer vase
(22-6″), 6 3/8″ by 3 3/4″.

$250-$275

Zephyr Lily flaring vase
(136-9″), 9 3/8″ by 5 1/2″.

$325-$375

Zephyr Lily handled wall pocket
unmarked, 8 1/8″ by 5 3/4″ by 2 5/8″.

$325-$375

Two green Zephyr Lily vases
136-9″ with repair to rim chip, and 140-12″, both marked.

$250-$300/pair

Pair of Zephyr Lily green vases
(135-9″), raised marks.

$200-$250/pair

Zephyr Lily green cornucopia vase
(203-6″), raised mark, grinding marks to base, 6 1/4″ by 5″ by 4 3/4″.

$150-$175

Pair of Zephyr Lily green wall pockets
(1297-8″), nick to tip of one, both marked.

$200-$250/pair

Other Patterns

Blue umbrella stand,
unmarked, 20" by 10".

$425-$475

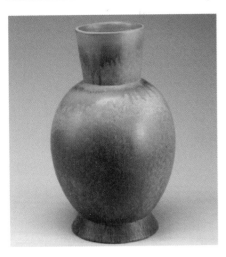

Carnelian form vase
with an Earlam glaze, unmarked, 18 1/4" by 10 1/2".

$3,200-$3,300

Jardinière
with three buttresses, 8 1/2" crack from rim, marked "468," 9 3/4" by 12".

$200-$250

Jardinière
covered in a cobalt matte glaze, unmarked, 9" tall.

$400-$450

Lamp base
with leaves that form small handles, restoration to one handle, original fittings, rare; pottery only: 10 1/4" tall.

$600-$700

Two pieces in the modern style:
one in dark blue (Rozane Pattern form, 3-8") and one turquoise with dark line to one handle; the second piece is unmarked, 12" tall.

$200- $250/pair

Wall pocket
in a mirrored blue glaze, minute fleck to hole, 9 3/4".

$90-$110

Other Roseville lines not pictured

Azurine-Orchid-Turquoise, early 1920s, is a line made up of Rosecraft shapes commonly seen in the Lustre line; solid colors of pale blue-green and pink, and no marks.

Blue/Black Teapots, early 1920s, include eight shapes. The black examples are unadorned, while the blue pots have small white floral decoration and gilt pinstripes; unmarked.

Cal Art, early 1950s, was a line of utilitarian pieces and planters in soft tones of blue, gray, green, yellow, and white, marked "Cal Art Creation" with a shape number, or "Created for Cal Art by Roseville U.S.A." with a shape number.

Chocolate Sets, circa 1912, included a 2-quart chocolate pot, milk pitcher, teapot, creamer, and sugar bowl. The transfer-decorated pieces featured a cherry motif, water lilies, grains, and assorted flowers. They are unmarked.

Colonial Set, circa 1905, was a sponge-decorated line of utility wares with a heavy embossed decoration and gilt trim in a late Victorian style. Pieces included a basin and pitcher, chamber pots, and small vessels, in colors of blue, brown, green, white, and yellow.

The Cornelian Line, circa 1900, was another Victorian-style group, also sponge-decorated, that included toilet sets, mixing bowls and serving vessels, and decorated pitchers in a rustic style. Some glazes followed the raised decorations, while others featured blue and brown sponging, with irregularly spaced gilt spattering and trim. Figural banks were included in this line.

Pasadena Planters, from 1954, were being made just months before Roseville ceased production. Many came with fitted metal bases, and colors included dark and light green, salmon, and pink. Many examples have raised marks.

Reproductions

Magnolia blue
(?) planter, faint and illegible raised mark, unusually heavy body and sloppy glaze, probably a reproduction, 7" by 5 1/4" by 3 1/4".

Real Jonquil squat vessel,
left, and a fake Jonquil bud vase, 6 1/2" tall, with a spurious Roseville raised mark, right.